collezionemaramotti

# ruby onyinyechi amanze

# HOW TO BE ENOUGH

Mousse Publishing

# SPACE AS/AND ICONOGRAPHY

Mario Diacono

Drawing is the initial stance of painting as it emerges in history, the initial birth of re-presentation: of a fragment or an aspect or an event of the world; with it, history essentially begins. It's with such awareness that ruby onyinyechi amanze makes drawing the exclusive medium of her artistic practice. It's her way to begin another story. Other artists, Francesco Clemente for instance, reclaimed between the late 1970s and the early 1980s—at the end of the minimalist, post-minimalist, and conceptual decade—the intention of painting from drawing; yet, amanze does not seem interested in following this path. She elevates drawing to painting, uses paper instead of canvas as a support for the media of painting, and not only because paper anticipated the arrival of canvas but also because paper becomes for her a subsequent phase, the phase in which painting acquires its own initiality. The intervention on the paper's surface of eventual incidents as reliefs that eliminate its flatness can be an implicit, or even explicit, invocation or evocation of the support that historically came in advance of painting—the rough surface of the rocks at Lascaux and Altamira.

The mini- and mytho-narrative of *HOW TO BE ENOUGH*, 2020, choreographed over fifteen paper panels of similar but not uniform height (approximately 310 centimeters) but vastly differing widths which entirely cover the 17.80 meters of the gallery's central wall, intuitively associate the work with the painted walls of medieval churches or Renaissance palaces, where painters with varying degrees of expressive invention frescoed sacred or profane legends and stories, and where the dimensions of the wall determined those of the work. The fifteen different iconic segments of *HOW TO BE ENOUGH*, in their constant variation of size and image, seem indeed to allude to dance steps articulating and traversing the wall/stage where the drawing unfolds. Drawing as choreographic action: the alternately figural and abstract movement in the work's representation is physically *performed* like a cinematic sequence of painted sheets of paper. In amanze's practice, however, the term "drawing" designates the type of support and surface, the paper, rather than the multiplicity of mediums to which the artist resorts in her work. Dance as a ritual element that underlies the fragmented narration of *HOW TO BE ENOUGH* is also symbolically alluded to, and included, in the movement of the five human figures that move along the sequence of the paper panels, from left to right: two diving women suspended in the aerial flight of a backward dive, the first arching leftward, at center, the second arching rightward, for almost the full height of the sheet; a third diving woman, forming a triangle with her body in a forward jackknife dive, occupies the upper left corner of the seventh sheet; a dancing female figure, clad from chest to feet in an enveloping white and black & gray striped garment, also takes over almost the entire size of the sheet; while in the final sheet a male diver is suspended, high up above the blue of a swimming pool, in the perfectly horizontal moment when he has lifted off the invisible diving board into the void. The first female in the backward dive is preceded by an empty sheet of white paper and is followed by a panel with two motor scooters which is in turn followed by two almost empty panels marked only by abstract blue elements. The sheets with the two other female divers, one very wide and with another backward dive, the other quite narrow and with the jackknife dive, are followed by a glass wall arched at the top and painted in a magenta color which rises up for almost the entire height of the sheet. After this come two sheets occupied by a single, blue polygonal swimming pool that zigzags through seven sides. In the eleventh sheet, the female dancer with the white and black striped garment raises her bent right arm upward while extending her left arm downward, a gesture with evident ritual implications, followed by a white sheet, then by a sheet with a one-story building drawn vertically and by another white sheet with a corner of a swimming pool wedged in its lower right. The rest of the large swimming pool inhabits the lower half of the last sheet and, high up above the deep-blue water, the male diver with a leopard face is flying, the perfect, eternal horizontality of his dive seeming to want to penetrate forever an outer space.

The dominant iconography of the work is the diving, of female and male divers counterpointed, in the spatial dynamic of the individual sheets, by other figures anchored to the ground: the scooters, the architectures, the swimming pools, the female dancer. Diving as the central theme of *HOW TO BE ENOUGH* introduces a dual level of significations, formal and metaphorical. Formally, the dive establishes an essential thematic role for both the divers and the space in tension between them and the water, a role that the space plays not subordinately but dialectically to that of the figures. Metaphorically, being airborne summons a notion of transcendence, which assimilates the divers to the archetype of saints and angels in medieval frescoes. By counterpointing, in the 17.80

meters of the representation, the four divers suspended in mid air with the figures on the ground—the dancer, the architectures, the massive pool at the work's extreme right—amanze choreographs the space as an essential iconic, or better iconographic component of the total image. The two scooters diagonally inscribed on the left as if they were taking off and the shaped form of the pool suspended in air at the center of the work further contribute, together with the four empty or almost empty sheets at the beginning and end of the paper fresco, to the fluidity, to the sense of spatial transcendence that connote *HOW TO BE ENOUGH*. This was, moreover, the basic tension in amanze's earlier works in which she also proves to be an extraordinary, classic drafts(wo)man, although of subjects that reference Ife's sculpture rather than Renaissance's visual culture. In amanze's drawings, archetypes and icons of African ascendance converse and collide with figures from today's Western society appropriated from American magazines, in a symbiotic and symbolic, and yet non-narrative, relationship of cultural evocations. The space in these drawings is never realistic, ignores perspective, is merely the space of the paper in its four directions, up down right left, north south east west, even if the representation, also not realistic, opens itself up to complete legibility. Coexisting in the space in a purely mental way, the figures avoid obeying any principle of gravity. In *The Divers*, 2016, for instance, two male divers go straight down on the upper left of the sheet: their perfectly vertical bodies have arms and legs covered with undefined geometric designs, in between bathing suits and tribal tattoos. Potted plants fly like birds on the upper right while, at center, up in the air as a flying carpet, there is a figure whose face echoes Ife's portraits but whose body is composite: two naked arms aim downward, hands touching the arch of an architectural structure similar to the magenta one in *HOW TO BE ENOUGH*, but, instead of legs, two arms covered in a denim jacket's sleeves stretch forward horizontally, the hands ritually turned one upward, the other down. Inserted on the chest of this figure with double arms but no legs is the head of a leopard, identifying him as *audre*, while on the lower left edge of the sheet two abstract geometric forms seem to allude to a sea and a sky. The largely white area below *audre* the leopard man, occupied only by the architectural drawing, dialectically defines the spatial/figural iconography of the image.

The artist has given a (sub)title to each of the fifteen sheets of *HOW TO BE ENOUGH*, clarifying or classifying the role that the individual figures have in the work's spatial/narrative sequence. The (sub)titles are not meant to be descriptive but rather allude to the conceptual sense that generated the image or that is being assigned to it.

The glosses/captions that are thus appended to the individual sheets, with language that intentionally borders on the poetic, further weld the spatial iconography to the figural one, rendering them in some way complementary. They also make it possible to associate the meaning of the images of *HOW TO BE ENOUGH* to that of many earlier drawings, revealing in the artist the recurring presence of a personal mythology in which figures and objects acquire symbolic value and become kind of hypostases of the interiority or the intellectuality of the artist. For instance, the Nigerian motor scooters, inscribed through photo transfer, also appear in the drawing *that low hanging sun*, 2016, as instances of social presentness connecting two headless leopard-men (or men tattooed with leopard skin) to a bodyless female head that emerges from a pattern of lines uniting a quasi-constellation of points/birds. This may perhaps also be a mechanical metaphor for *ada* and *audre*, the names of the couple recurring both in the glosses of *HOW TO BE ENOUGH* and in the artist's vast body of conceptual narratives. *ada* is mentioned in four of these glosses:

2 (backward dive)
*OUT. SHE EXITED QUIETLY, BUT DECIDEDLY*
or *[ada] edge, left*

6 (backward dive)
*OVERRIDING*
*[she was wild]* or *the first. [ada].*

7 (forward jackknife dive)
*IT WAS FROM WATER. TO WATER, WE RETURN.*
or *[ada] top, dives*

11 (female dancer)
*AS GRACE [Judith] SHE ASKED, WHAT COLOR IS*
*A WINDOW? MY DARLING, A WINDOW IS CLEAR*
*OR IT'S PINK.*
and/or *[ada + windows] up. down.*

while *audre* is named in the last subtitle:

15 (horizontal male diver)
*THE EXPANSE OF AUDRE [EASE OF FLIGHT]*

*[DEPTH] wings fueled by generators and palm wine,*
*audre holds us up*
and/or *[audre + pool #2] above and beneath*

The backward divers in turn recall the female swimmer in *Starfish*, 2016. In the glosses, the name *ada* recurs, designating a female diver and a dancer, while the name *audre* appears once, denoting the male/leopard diver suspended in air in the final sheet. The (sub)title that offers commentary for the forward jackknife diver in the seventh sheet, *IT WAS FROM WATER. TO WATER, WE RETURN*, possibly alludes to another, different key for understanding the work, ascribing to it a metaphysical dimension. *ada+audre* appear earlier, in a 2015 drawing with the same title, while *audre* appears in a drawing from that same year, *18 kisses at a beach with a hammock for audre [to learn to pray]*. In this latter work, *audre*, who is almost always a present-day person with a male body but the head of a leopard (perhaps signifying the unity of Africa and Europe in the artist's visual culture; but it should also be remembered that the Nigerian Oba, the king of Benin, is symbolically compared to a leopard and, for this reason, a tamed leopard was always present at the Oba court), kneels praying in a hammock suspended in space. The hammock is wedged between a couple standing above (a female figure—*ada*?) embraced by a naked green man whose headdress recalls an African tribal mask, and a couple seated on the ground below, kissing in a tight embrace. In *ada+audre*, 2015, the two figures are tightly dancing, *ada* wearing a light blue garment, her hair gathered into a monumental African hairdo, *audre* in a gray double-breasted suit and with a leopard's head, their heads surrounded by an ocher oval halo. While the name *ada* is a palindrome that, in its simplicity, can live in different languages and cultures (but it's also the name of one of the two ceremonial swords, *ada* and *eben*, that the Oba traditionally carried as symbols of his powers), *audre* is an English female name that the artist might have adopted from Audre Lorde (1934–1992), an Afro-American poetess and political activist; it could, however, also be derived from the French *autre*, to express the existential otherness that connotes the artist's Blackness.

In his different incarnations, *audre* changes form and clothing but always has the partially theriomorphic aspect of a supernatural being. In *HOW TO BE ENOUGH*, in addition to a diver's bathing suit, the figure wears only a leopard's face and, remaining suspended midair in a completely horizontal position seems to suggest the nature of a divine aviator.

The classicism in amanze's drawings, that informs many of the heads that appear either isolated or as attributes of improbable figures, male or female, comes directly from African classic sculpture which historians have now recognized in the portraits produced at the court of the Nigerian Oni (kings) of Ife (fourteenth–sixteenth century?) to maintain the memory of deceased court personages. While European modernists of the early twentieth century enthusiastically embraced African tribal sculptures as archetypes in their search for increasingly expressive or even expressionistic forms, the progressive modernism practiced by amanze, a different, alternative one, a Eurafrican modernism inspired by Ife's sculptures, aims to an art where, to quote Mortimer Wheeler defining the Nigerian artistic experience, "the sense of rhythm and of theater" is still strong. With her composite/complex Euro-African modernism, amanze retraces naturally the Blackness of Ife as a metaphor for history as an eternal present. Her *mise en oeuvre* of an anti-gravitational spatiality within which fluctuate in equal measure, with collagistic modalities, figural inventions—ranging from the abstract to the grotesque and from the architectural to the fantastic—and visual quotations drawn from the mass media (maybe also from the visual vocabulary of science fiction) abolishes in the representation any temporal and figural distance between past, present, and future.

Regarding the title, *HOW TO BE ENOUGH* is the work's response both to the question that art poses to the artist personally—about the media she uses, the visual culture from which and within which she moves and to which she reacts—and to the question that is posed to the artist socially as a person of color—a question that weighs existentially on her practice, and not only in the United States. This is how amanze has explained it:

"The title is a nod to paper, drawing, and minimalism. Both the physical medium, and the larger context and histories . . . The secondary part of where the title came from, is what it means to do all of the above while being Black in America . . . in short, I perceive limitations on what Black artists can or should create. 'They' [the market? the collector?] want to see the figure. Portraiture. Color. Paint.

I'm making the drawings that I make."

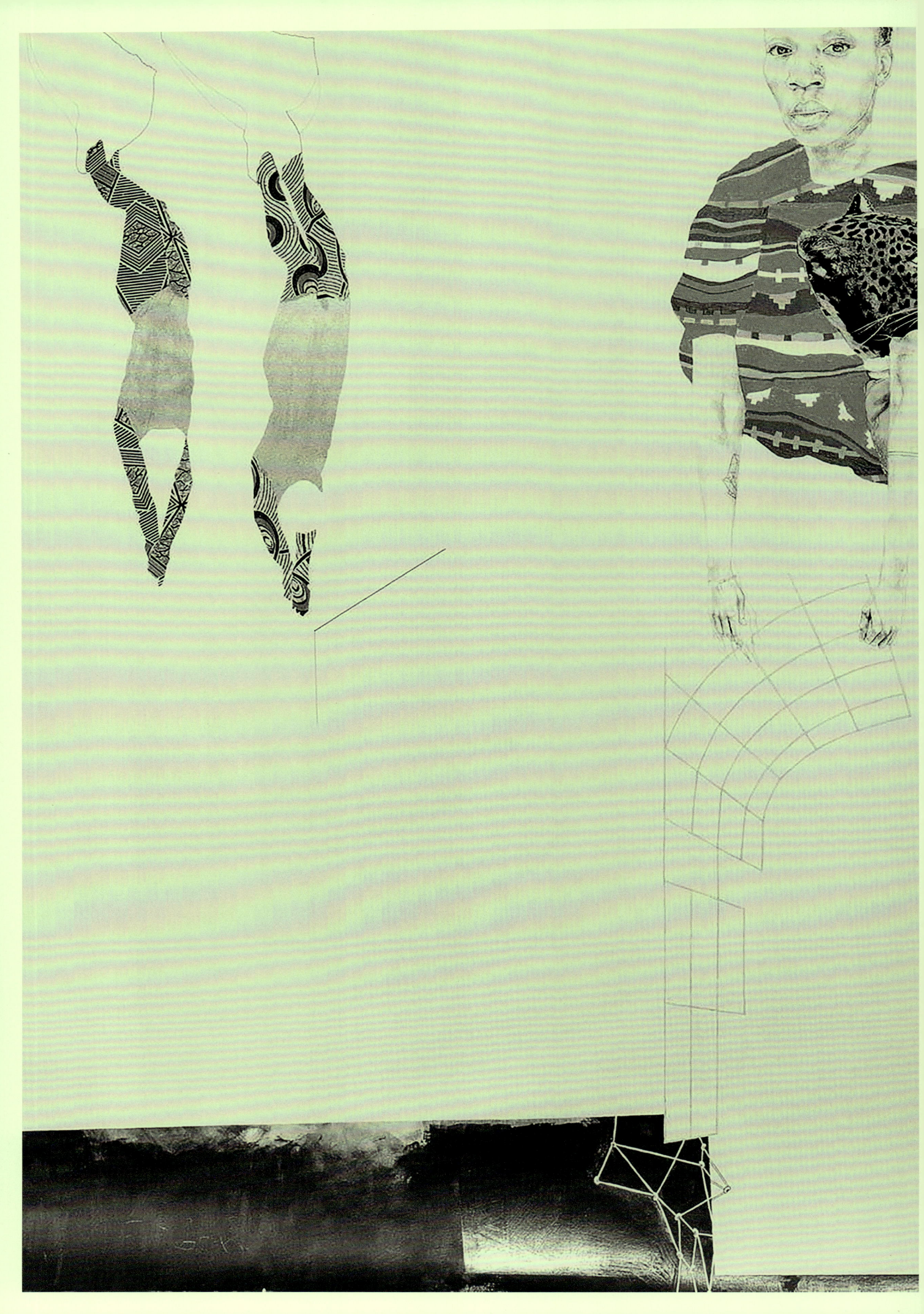

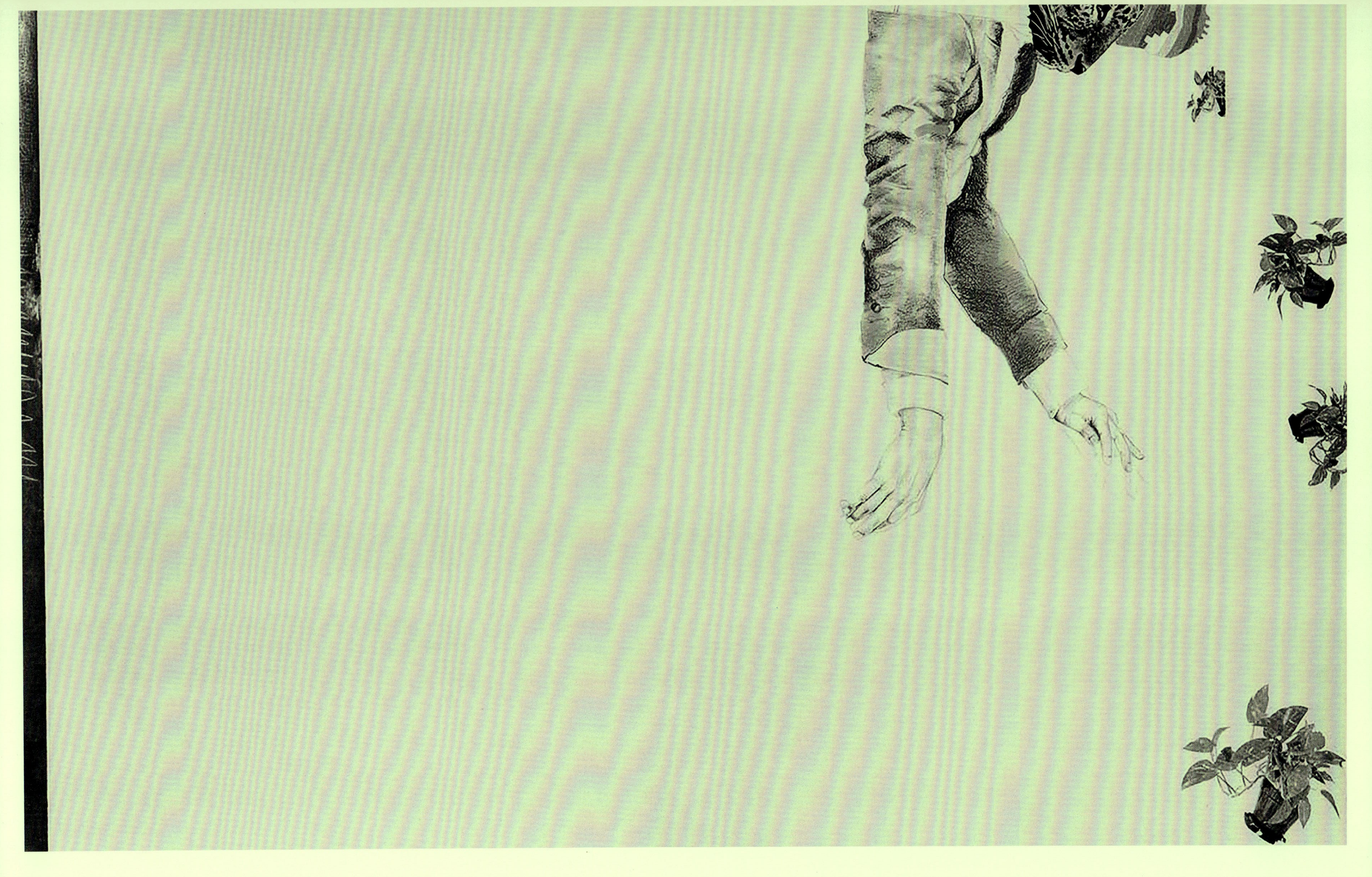

*The Divers*, 2016

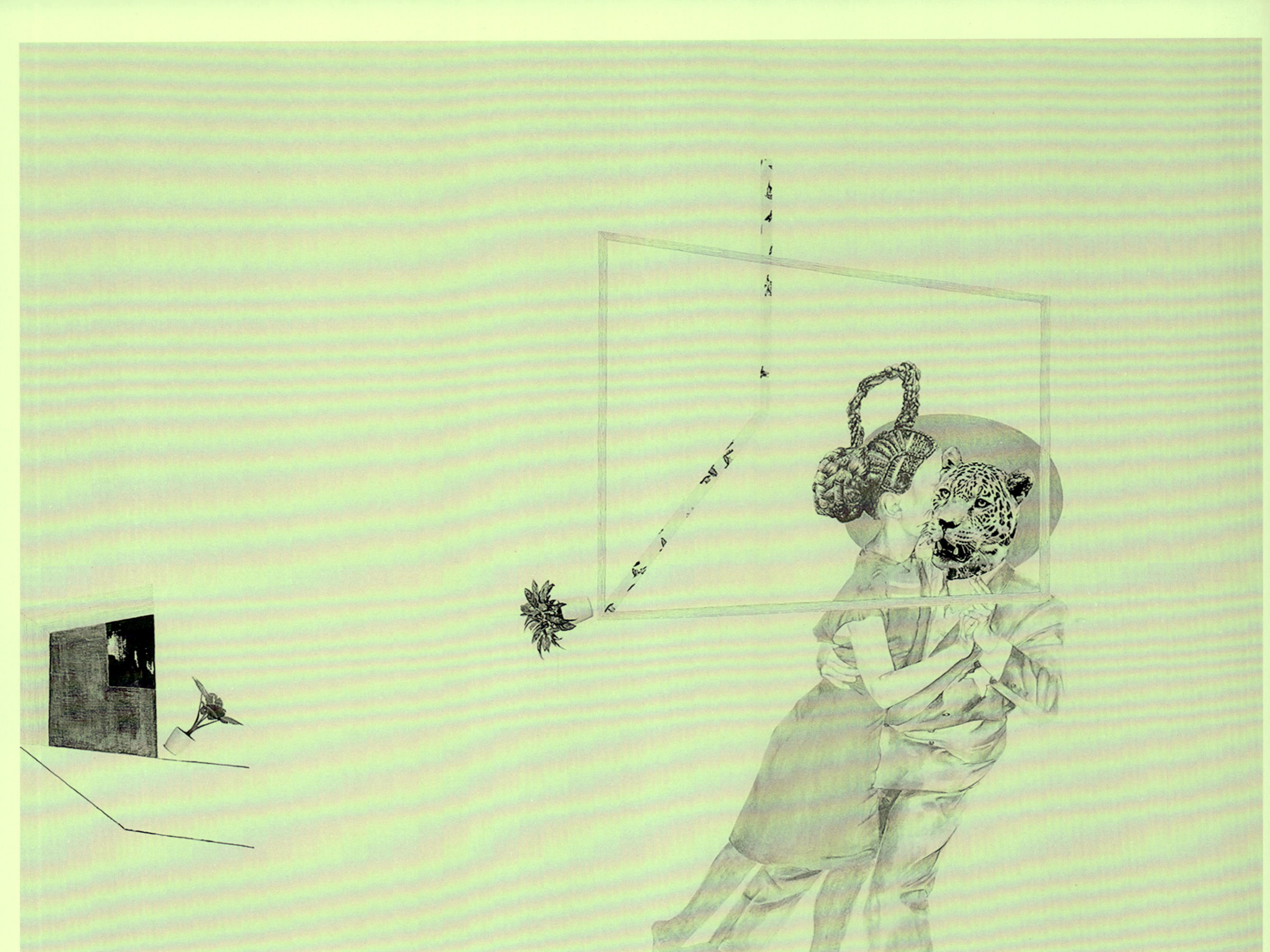

*ada+audre*, 2015

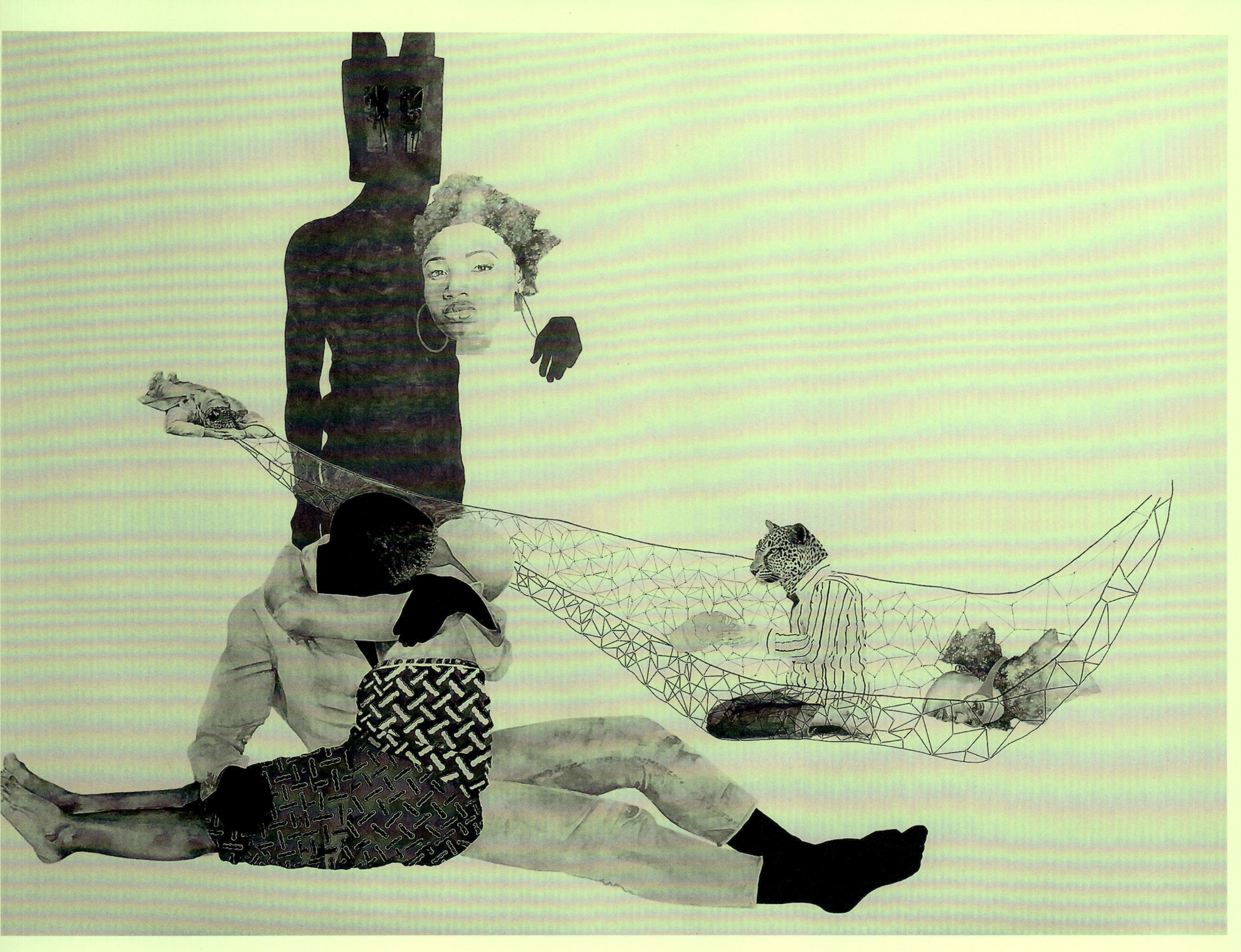

*18 kisses at a beach with a hammock for audre [to learn to pray]*, 2015

# SPAZIO E/COME ICONOGRAFIA

Mario Diacono

Il disegno è il momento iniziale della pittura nel suo emergere alla storia: il momento iniziale della rappresentazione di un frammento o un aspetto o un evento del mondo con cui effettivamente la storia inizia. Con questa consapevolezza, ruby onyinyechi amanze fa del disegno lo strumento esclusivo della sua pratica artistica. È il modo di iniziare un'altra storia. Altri artisti, Francesco Clemente per esempio, tra la fine degli anni Settanta e gli inizi degli anni Ottanta, alla fine del decennio minimalista, post-minimalista e concettuale ripresero dal disegno l'intenzione della pittura; amanze non sembra interessata a ripetere questo percorso. amanze eleva il disegno a pittura, usa la carta anziché la tela come supporto ai media della pittura, non solo perché la carta anticipa l'arrivo della tela, la carta diventa per lei anzi una fase successiva, la fase in cui la pittura riacquista la sua inizialità. Il suo incidentare la superficie della carta con eventuali rilievi che ne eliminino la piattezza può essere un'implicita, forse anche esplicita, invocazione o evocazione del supporto storicamente primo della pittura, la superficie scabra delle rocce di Lascaux e Altamira.

La mini- e mito-narrativa di *HOW TO BE ENOUGH*, 2020, coreografata su quindici pannelli di carta di altezza simile ma non uniforme, 310 centimetri circa, e di larghezze invece ampiamente diverse, che ricoprono interamente i 17,80 metri della parete centrale della galleria, associa intuitivamente il lavoro ai muri dipinti delle chiese del Medioevo o dei palazzi del Rinascimento, dove pittori di maggiore o minore espressività affrescavano mitologie sacre o profane, e dove le dimensioni della parete determinavano quelle dell'opera. I quindici diversi segmenti iconici di *HOW TO BE ENOUGH*, nella costante variazione di misura e di immagine, sembrano anche alludere a passi di danza che scandiscano e percorrano la "scena" in cui il disegno si dispiega. Disegno come azione coreografica: il movimento alternativamente figurale e astratto nella rappresentazione viene fisicamente *performed* come sequenza cinematica di fogli di carta dipinti. Il termine "disegno" designa tuttavia, nelle opere di amanze, più il tipo di supporto e di superficie, la carta, che non i molteplici media di cui l'artista fa uso nella rappresentazione. La danza come elemento rituale che sottende la frammentata narrazione di *HOW TO BE ENOUGH* viene simbolicamente allusa e inclusa nel movimento delle cinque figure umane che percorrono la sequenza dei fogli: da sinistra a destra, due tuffatrici sospese nel volo aereo di un tuffo all'indietro, la prima inarcata verso sinistra al centro del foglio, la seconda inarcata verso destra, per quasi l'intera grandezza del foglio; una terza tuffatrice, piegata a formare col corpo un triangolo nel suo tuffo in avanti carpiato, occupa l'angolo in alto a sinistra del settimo foglio; una figura femminile danzante, con un voluminoso abito a strisce bianche e nere/grigie che la veste dal petto ai piedi, occupa anch'essa quasi l'intero foglio; nell'ultimo foglio, un tuffatore è sospeso in alto sopra l'azzurro di una piscina, nel momento perfettamente orizzontale in cui ha lasciato il trampolino all'inizio del salto nel vuoto. La prima tuffatrice con un tuffo all'indietro, preceduta da un foglio di carta bianco vuoto, è seguita da un pannello con due moto scooter e da due pannelli quasi vuoti, segnati da elementi astratti azzurri; i fogli con due altre tuffatrici, uno molto largo con un tuffo anch'esso all'indietro, l'altro molto stretto con il tuffo carpiato, sono seguiti da una vetrata color magenta curva in alto, che si alza per quasi l'intera superficie del foglio; vengono poi due fogli con una piscina poligonale azzurra che zigzaga per sette lati. Nell'undicesimo foglio, la danzatrice con l'abito a strisce bianche e nere alza il braccio destro piegato verso l'alto e stende il braccio sinistro verso il basso, un gesto con chiare implicazioni rituali; la seguono un foglio bianco, un foglio con un edificio a un solo piano presentato però verticalmente, e un foglio bianco in cui s'incunea in basso a destra il lato di una piscina. Il resto della piscina occupa gran parte dell'ultimo foglio, la sorvola in estrema lontananza il tuffatore la cui totale, permanente orizzontalità sembra voler penetrare uno spazio infinito.

Iconografia dominante dell'opera appare quella del tuffo, tuffatori/tuffatrici, contrappuntati nella dinamica spaziale dei singoli fogli dalle istanze di figure ancorate a terra: gli scooter, le architetture, le piscine, la danzatrice. Il tuffo, il tuffarsi come tema centrale di *HOW TO BE ENOUGH* importa un doppio livello di significazione, formale e metaforica. Formalmente il tuffo istituisce un ruolo figurale essenziale sia alle tuffatrici che allo spazio in tensione tra tuffatore/tuffatrici e l'acqua, un ruolo dialettico, non subalterno a quello delle figure umane. Metaforicamente l'essere *airborne* intima una nozione di trascendenza, che assimila i *divers* agli archetipi dei santi e angeli negli affreschi medievali. Contrappuntando nei 17,80 metri della rappresentazione i quattro tuffatori sospesi in volo con la danzatrice a terra, le architetture verticali, e la massiccia piscina all'estrema destra dell'opera, amanze coreografa così lo spazio come un'essenziale componente iconica, o meglio iconografica, dell'immagine totale. I due scooter inscritti diagonalmente sulla sinistra, come se stessero decollando, la forma poligonale della piscina sospesa a mezz'aria al centro contribuiscono ulteriormente, con i quattro fogli vuoti o quasi vuoti verso l'inizio e la fine dell'affresco in carta, alla fluidità e al senso di trascendenza spaziale che connotano *HOW TO BE ENOUGH*. Questa è stata del resto la fondamentale tensione nei precedenti lavori dell'artista, nei quali amanze si dimostra fra l'altro straordinaria, classica disegnatrice anche se di soggetti che referenziano la cultura visuale di Ife anziché quella rinascimentale europea. Nei suoi disegni, archetipi e iconi di ascendenza africana conversano e collidono con figure della cronaca d'oggi appropriate dai rotocalchi americani, in una relazione simbolica e simbiotica, non-narrativa, di pura evocazione culturale. In questi disegni lo spazio non è mai realistico, ignora la prospettiva, è lo spazio puro del foglio nelle sue quattro direzioni, alto basso destra sinistra, e la rappresentazione, pur non essendo nemmeno essa realistica, si apre a una completa leggibilità. Convivendo nello spazio in modo puramente mentale, le figure evitano di obbedire al principio di gravitazione. In *The Divers*, 2016, per esempio, due tuffatori scendono a picco sulla sinistra alta del foglio: i loro corpi perfettamente verticali hanno braccia e gambe coperte da disegni geometrici incerti tra costumi da bagno e tatuaggi tribali. In alto a destra volano come uccelli vasi di piante, e al centro è sospesa in alto una figura il cui viso echeggia le sculture di Ife ma il cui corpo è composito: due braccia nude volte in basso le cui mani toccano l'arco di una struttura architettonica simile a quella di *HOW TO BE ENOUGH*, mentre al posto delle gambe si distendono orizzontalmente in avanti due braccia coperte dalle maniche di una giacca, con le mani ritualmente volte una verso l'alto, l'altra verso il basso. Sul petto di questa figura con doppie braccia ma senza gambe s'innesta una testa di leopardo, identificandolo come *audre*, mentre all'estremità in basso a sinistra del foglio due forme geometriche astratte sembrano alludere a un mare e a un cielo. L'area bianca intermedia, occupata al centro solo dal disegno architettonico, definisce dialetticamente l'iconografia spaziale dell'immagine.

A ciascuno dei quindici fogli di *HOW TO BE ENOUGH* l'artista ha dato un suo (sotto)titolo, il quale puntualizza il ruolo che le singole figure hanno nella sequenza spaziale/narrativa dell'opera. I (sotto)titoli non vogliono essere descrittivi, alludono piuttosto al momento concettuale che ha generato l'immagine o che le viene assegnato.

Le glosse/didascalie che l'artista appone, con linguaggio al limite del poetico, ai singoli fogli saldano così ulteriormente l'iconografia spaziale a quella figurale rendendole in qualche modo complementari. Esse permettono inoltre di omologare il senso delle immagini di *HOW TO BE ENOUGH* a quello di diversi dei disegni precedenti, rivelando nell'artista la presenza ricorrente di una mitologia personale in cui figure e oggetti acquistano valore simbolico e diventano ipostasi dell'interiorità o dell'intellettualità dell'artista stessa. I moto scooter nigeriani, inscritti mediante photo transfer, appaiono per esempio in *that low hanging sun*, 2016, quali istanze di realtà sociale colleganti due uomini-leopardo (o tatuati) senza testa a una testa femminile senza corpo che emerge da un reticolo di linee che uniscono una quasi-costellazione di punti/uccelli, o forse anche come metafore meccaniche di *ada* e *audre*, i nomi della coppia ricorrente sia nelle glosse di *HOW TO BE ENOUGH* che nella vasta narrativa concettuale dell'artista. *ada* è menzionata in quattro di tali glosse:

2 (tuffo all'indietro)
*OUT. SHE EXITED QUIETLY, BUT DECIDEDLY*
or *[ada] edge, left*

6 (tuffo all'indietro)
*OVERRIDING*
*[she was wild]* or *the first. [ada].*

7 (tuffo in avanti carpiato)
*IT WAS FROM WATER. TO WATER, WE RETURN.*
or *[ada] top, dives*

11 (danzatrice)
*AS GRACE [Judith] SHE ASKED, WHAT COLOR IS A WINDOW? MY DARLING, A WINDOW IS CLEAR OR IT'S PINK.*
and/or *[ada + windows] up. down.*

mentre *audre* viene nominato nell'ultimo sottotitolo:

15 (tuffatore orizzontale)
*THE EXPANSE OF AUDRE [EASE OF FLIGHT] [DEPTH] wings fueled by generators and palm wine, audre holds us up*
and/or *[audre + pool #2] above and beneath*

La tuffatrice all'indietro richiama inoltre la nuotatrice di *Starfish*, 2016. Nelle glosse il nome *ada* ricorre a designare una tuffatrice e una volta la danzatrice, mentre il nome *audre* appare una volta per nominare il tuffatore sospeso in aria nell'ultimo foglio. Il (sotto)titolo che commenta il tuffo carpiato in avanti, nel settimo foglio, *IT WAS FROM WATER. TO WATER, WE RETURN* (È COMINCIATO DALL'ACQUA. ALL'ACQUA RITORNIAMO) sembra inoltre alludere a una delle diverse, possibili chiavi di lettura dell'opera, inscrivendovi una dimensione metafisica. *ada+audre* emergono già in un disegno dallo stesso titolo del 2015, mentre *audre* appare in un disegno dello stesso anno, *18 kisses at a beach with a hammock for audre [to learn to pray]*. In quest'ultimo, *audre*, che è quasi sempre un personaggio attuale con corpo maschile ma la testa di leopardo (forse a significare l'indissolubilità di Africa ed Europa nella cultura visiva dell'artista, ma va anche ricordato che al leopardo veniva simbolicamente comparato l'Oba nigeriano, il re di Benin, e per questo un leopardo domesticato era sempre presente nella corte degli Oba), è inginocchiato e prega dentro un'amaca sospesa nello spazio, incuneata tra una coppia in piedi in alto (una figura femminile – *ada*?) abbracciata da una figura maschile nuda verde la cui testa è costituita da una forma che richiama una maschera tribale africana e una coppia seduta a terra in basso, stretta in un abbraccio amoroso. In *ada+audre*, 2015, le due figure sono strette in un abbraccio di danza, *ada* con un abito celeste e i capelli raccolti in una monumentale acconciatura africana, *audre* in un vestito a doppio petto grigio e la testa di leopardo, le loro teste circondate da un'aureola ovale ocra. Mentre il nome *ada* è un palindromo che nella sua semplicità può apparire in lingue e culture diverse (ma è anche il nome di una delle due spade cerimoniali, *ada* e *eben*, che tradizionalmente gli Oba portavano come simbolo del loro potere), *audre* è un nome femminile inglese che l'artista potrebbe avere adottato da quello di Audre Lorde (1934-1992), una poetessa e attivista politica afro-americana. Esso potrebbe essere tuttavia derivato anche dalla parola francese *autre*, per esprimere l'alterità esistenziale che connota la Blackness dell'artista.

Nelle sue diverse apparizioni, *audre* cambia forma e abbigliamento ma ha sempre l'aspetto parzialmente teriomorfico di un essere soprannaturale. In *HOW TO BE ENOUGH* indossa solo, oltre al costume da bagno di tuffatore, la testa di leopardo, e nel restare sospeso in aria in posizione totalmente orizzontale sembra proporre in sé la natura di un aviatore divino. Il classicismo dei disegni di amanze, che informa molti dei visi che appaiono isolati o come attributi di improbabili figure maschili o femminili, proviene direttamente dalla classicità africana ormai riconosciuta dagli storici nella scultura prodotta alla corte degli Oni (re) nigeriani di Ife (XIV-XVI secolo?) come ritrattistica di personaggi defunti. Mentre i modernisti europei degli inizi del XX secolo si entusiasmavano delle sculture tribali africane quali archetipi nella loro ricerca di forme sempre più espressive o magari espressioniste, il modernismo progressivo praticato da amanze, un modernismo ulteriore, euro-africano, si ispira decisamente alle sculture di Ife per un'arte dove sia forte "il senso del ritmo e del teatro", nelle parole di Mortimer Wheeler, che connotava l'esperienza artistica nigeriana. In tale composito/complesso modernismo euro-africano, si innesta con naturalezza la Blackness di Ife come metafora di una storia quale eterno presente, la *mise en oeuvre* di una spazialità antigravitazionale, dentro la quale fluttuano in eguale misura, con modalità collagistiche, invenzioni figurali – che vanno dall'astratto al grottesco, dall'architettonico al fantastico – e citazioni visuali tratte dai media di massa, forse anche dal vocabolario visivo della fantascienza, abolendo nella rappresentazione ogni distanza temporale e figurale tra passato, presente e futuro.

Quanto al titolo, *HOW TO BE ENOUGH* è la risposta dell'opera sia alla domanda che l'arte le pone personalmente: sui media che usa, sulla cultura visuale da cui ed entro cui si muove e a cui reagisce; sia alla domanda sociale che viene posta oggi all'artista come persona di colore – una domanda che incide esistenzialmente sulla sua pratica, e non solo negli Stati Uniti. amanze ha spiegato così il titolo:

*"The title is a nod to paper, drawing, and minimalism. Both the physical medium, and the larger context and histories . . . The secondary part of where the title came from, is what it means to do all of the above while being Black in America . . . in short, I perceive limitations on what Black artists can or should create. 'They' [the market? the collector?] want to see the figure. Portraiture. Color. Paint.*

*I'm making the drawings that I make".**

* Il titolo è un'allusione alla carta, al disegno, al minimalismo. Sia a ciascuno come medium fisico che al più vasto loro contesto e alle storie che questo implica... L'altra allusione a cui il titolo rimanda è: cosa significhi fare questo lavoro per chi è Black in America... in altre parole, sento che vengono poste limitazioni a quello che gli artisti Black possono o dovrebbero creare. Loro [il mercato? il collezionista?] vogliono vedere la figura. Ritratti. Colore. Pittura.

Io faccio i disegni che faccio.

# "AND SOMETHING ABOUT BEAUTY." SOME CORRESPONDENCE WITH RUBY ONYINYECHI AMANZE

Gaia Clotilde Chernetich

This text was born from an exercise of imagination and from a proposal. I asked ruby onyinyechi amanze to become pen pals. Now I read it as an exchange anchored in a mutual and affectionate openness. Unexpected. We used the letter as a revealing tool, we dived and danced. Now it is time to pass on these thoughts to our future readers.

03.12.21

Dear Ruby,

after the video call where we decided to start this correspondence, I tried to recall the feelings of my last visit to Collezione Maramotti. It was a few months before the pandemic. It is surprising to know that we were both present for Dimitris Papaioannou's site-specific performance. We have never met yet, but we already shared an experience that set a common temporal and spatial reference between us. I remember the silence and the special brightness of the space. The light was pastel that afternoon. I visited the galleries. I was looking forward to attending the performance. The presence of dance and performance art in exhibition spaces triggers many questions. I read about your dance practice and your interest in performance, could you please tell me more about this?

When it comes to thinking "how free" we are now, as human beings, I have no answers. I feel that the restrictions we are dealing with have the power to change the perspectives on ourselves; they surely have that power on me. Personally, I am finding my freedom in the most "restricted" part of me, my body. This may sound like an oxymoron, I know. But if there's a form of freedom, today, to me, it can only be as a form of resistance. I am not sure if it is a sort of resilience, instead. Is there a way to live in this "new-habitat," and create art without referring to our recent (and, apparently, already lost) past? Are we going to be a new kind of memory-based and past-dependent generation? Are we currently "suspended," waiting for being able to create a new relationship to our bodies and to our past/present/future?

The current situation with the coronavirus highlights our bodies' centrality. I am aware that the corporeal element is present in your artistic research. I think of your divers and dancers. Has your perspective on the body changed since the pandemic? How do you involve your own body in your art? Is it a starting point or a "place" where you develop something that emerged before, while drawing?

For us, I see the possibility to become a generation dealing with a permanent reference to past experiences, lived and archived in a suddenly lost set of time and space . . . I don't know if these ideas produce an echo in you and in your work but being myself part of the "next generation" of a diasporic community (my family left their homeland in Istria, in 1947, as refugees) I see many connections between the present we live in and another chapter of potential trauma to deal with.

Take care, dear Ruby

Gaia

03.17.21

*dearest Gaia, i want to say dearest, because even though i don't know you—this is intimacy. what we are doing. the way we are sharing. i like that it's that way and not one directional or authoritarian. from talking to you that day in the videocall it already felt right. to work on this together. and to approach it from the side and not from the front. in some ways i am direct. fixed like my sign [scorpio]. very clear on exactly the way i feel and the way i want things to be. but mostly, i float. and obscure. and am elusive. this is my nature. how do you move? what would they say of your essence?*

*and perhaps this is a rather simple question, but are you a dancer?*

*the body. you mentioned it. the restrictions of movement . . . of touch . . . of closeness. yes, i feel all of these things. one of my earliest formed and at this point, most concrete relationships i have with my body, is that of machine. i ran competitively for 2+ decades. i still would, if racing were permitted. i don't think of my body as mine necessarily. i mean, it is. but i am embodied within it. i am an alien. and i chose to enter it as a way to experience the world. it's necessary for certain things —like running. jumping in puddles. eating food and deciding if you (who is you?) appreciate the flavors. i trained my body. spoke to it as a distanced self. body—please do this thing. thank you, body.*

*i draw with it too. drawing is like running. i keep wanting to say that—talk about that—but it doesn't seem people are really listening.*

*i don't think it's changed for me. i mean, since the pandemic. and no, i don't want this to be centered in that conversation. i'm not sure what else there is to say when we are inside of it. maybe later? i wonder about five years in the future. this thing that happened. for me, it was subtle. i was not disrupted in catastrophic ways. subtle is dangerous too though. surely, my molecules have shifted, but i'm not sure yet the extent of the change. perhaps i am a bit numb. too close to normal to have adequate words to describe . . . this thing. i miss everything and everybody. that's what i say on the saddest days. the other days are __________. as for art, art survives everything doesn't it? performance too. i know it was hit harder than other mediums. or that the "pivot" was more visible, more necessary. some things don't translate though. the digital cannot breathe like we do. eyeballs on flesh emit energy that computer screens cannot. do you wait it out or do this other version? what if the other version is somehow against your core?*

*it's funny that we shared space at the Collezione Maramotti. did we stand next to each other? across the room? did you see me? i probably saw you. i am a deep scanner of rooms with people in them. i want to find secrets.*

*i like what you wrote about the generations. and being diasporic. i am too—not as a descendent of refugees, but as an immigrant. so, some part of me understands what it is to be in other lands. i've never quite understood how generations actually work. i have a child. but i think we are two generations apart. wouldn't it just be one? i think you're right . . . we'll approach our futures with this active memory of a past. many didn't celebrate birthdays last year—not that birthdays are accurate markers of anything real—but also, the year disappeared. fell off the face of the earth. was not accounted for. but was remembered in our blood. have i spoken too much of the thing i don't want to talk about? perhaps. can we issue a ban now? we've both gotten something off our chests. . .*

*what are the questions triggered by dance in museums? is it an issue of audience? or proximity? is it seen as problematic? everything is problematic. i am remembering the judson dance theater era in new york. or not remembering it per se, seeing as i wasn't born, but i feel aligned to it. all the conversations about spaces and galleries and dance as fine art and attempts to take the barriers down and access the people in more "authentic" ways. my friend wura hates how galleries try to squeeze out a performance from their artists at openings. as if gallery goers need to be entertained, because visual art isn't enough. or as if performance was a show to be passively consumed, like the television. neither are true.*

*i love architecture and the grounds at the Collezione Maramotti are incredible! i'm not sure where our dance will happen yet. we are created in a vacuum almost. between worlds. when we arrive, we must take it all apart. lay it bare. see how it feels in the rooms. in Reggio Emilia. will it travel well? we must get to know it [the dance] and ourselves almost from scratch. it will morph into a new creature. you cannot take something and put it somewhere else and expect for it to be the same thing.*

*in my drawings i'm inking these swimming pools and borrowing something from painting. still drawing, in part, because of the medium. as much as i'd love to resist [i'm pretty unapologetic about being a paint "hater"], i can't pretend that i'm not painterly in those moments. and truth be told, i love that my entry point is one of ignorance. or naivete. i can be honest like a child. new. exploratory. channeled by joy and clumsiness. imperfection. there's too much pressure towards mastery. dance is no exception. whole bones contorting into shapes that supposedly are better suited for doing a thing maybe bodies aren't supposed to do. what about all the moments before your body inputs the movement into your brain? what about bones that are too big or square when they should be round? and what if you want to stay in the curiosity and humility of not knowing? just for a while longer. why am i saying this? i was thinking about dance. and me. and my not being trained. my partner keeps asking if i'm an imposter. how i can reckon with myself by being a dancer now. "all of a sudden." it sounds worse than it is. i like to be challenged. . .*

*it's not all of a sudden though. it's forever. i have danced my whole life. and spent a lot of time in the past five years thinking, watching, reading, drawing, inhaling dance. i'm missing a lot. i don't carry the vigor in my muscles, like i don't carry paint and never will. i'm not in denial and i want to be able to talk about this. lean into it. see where it can take me/allow me to go. which doors can i open from this place? alongside Mor, who does have the memory. the accumulation of histories, training, context, language.*

*i've performed before. most quaky textural stuff. or solemn and endurance based. in performance work—most often i'm a body for another artist. rarely as my own concept/design. i love to move and to dance. perhaps you're familiar with the movement language of gaga? it was my joy when i lived in new york. i love to explore the tactility of space. that's what my drawings are ultimately about. it comes from being an immigrant, but that's just the beginning story of it. it's an old story now. maybe irrelevant even . . . but from moving and taking pieces of land or memory to make new pieces of land or memory. the gaps in between worlds. the division of the self into all the places the body has been. the overlaps and the way the sky bends. the way the water transmutes secrets.*

*and something about beauty.*

*that's the other part of movement for me. grace. the delicacy of tracing a line with your finger.*

*and of course, what is beauty without physicality? brute power. endurance. an utter lack of grace.*

*i feel as though i have so much to say but i am only saying the tiniest little bit. are you feeling me? am i making any sense? where do we go from here?*

*thank you for writing me. i do wish this were analogue. i am one for paper and pen.*

03.22.21

Dearest Ruby,

Rome's desert outside my window, people aren't tracing any choreography in the streets: we all walk, move, share less and less. Or, better said, we can share but separately. Anyway, today it is sunny and chilly, *spring-ish*. I went to the park with my son. The city seems anaesthetized. Again. It will soon be over, they say.

In this general context of separation(s), writing to you—reaching out to you, in the United States on the other side of the ocean—and talking about something of yours which is physically happening closer to me than to you . . . it creates a strange way of feeling space. Space is one of the keywords of these times. Do you think about space when you draw or when you prepare something to be exhibited? As a dance dramaturg (I'm a—former—dancer, yes!), space is something I deal with.

How do you see creativity? Does it directly involve dance in your work? I recently had a conversation regarding the idea of "being creative" with a friend of mine. To me, "being creative" is something that does not necessarily go with being an artist.

I am impressed when you write: "I don't think of my body as mine necessarily." This is a dancer's way of thinking! I have lived like this. Not because I was ever expropriated of my body, but because in order to *be* a dancer, I had to let other people's thoughts so deep in me that, sometimes, I could concretely feel the distance between *my-self* and *my-flesh*. Do you perhaps see a connection between your interest in dance and being a runner? Drawing is like running, you wrote.

Is there a story you want to express or narrate through your art? And, in this case, what kind of medium is your body? As a dancer, and even as a dance dramaturg and writer, I think there's no way to avoid narration. It may be not in your will or in your eyes, but the spectators' ones are made to make things understandable through vision, first of all. In this sense, as our eyes have such superpowers (they bring in images, don't they?), how do you involve your spectators in your work?

You're no impostor when you dance. Nobody can be an impostor while moving the body. Performance is everywhere. I am curious to know what you think about the boundaries between disciplines. Visual artists, performance artists, artivists, etc. From my point of view, all these categories are mixing and melting. And, at the same time, self-positioning is one of the most significant issues in the arts field.

Dance and museums or performances and galleries are common binomial. The never-ending question is: how do they affect each other? A lot has been written on this topic. What will be at stake in the future?

I wish we could now pour a coffee and continue this conversation face to face . . . and as I could go on writing and writing, I now force myself to stop and click send.

Thank you, Ruby.

Take care,

Gaia

04.01.21

*you have a child too! this made me smile. another strange adult human in partnership with another adult human who somehow—in whatever form or fashion—landing with a tiny human creature. just like me. just like billions before us and after us. yes, an odd way of interacting/not interacting for a little one to process. but they are the smartest of all of us. and things get erased in these early months on earth. or absorbed and disintegrated into the tiniest immeasurable fragments. for us too. we are already breaking this memory down as we live in. in real time, we are forgetting. masks? what masks? two years of life will shrink. with each passing year, i imagine it becoming less and less real. and two months of life will disappear entirely. but what do we actually know? maybe it was those first two months of life that mattered the most. that made us into who we are. i am prepared to fuck up as a parent. in lots of lovely ways. but the part i will do right is to line her base—her foundation—her default grounding place—with all the love i can muster. with all the affirmations i am needing myself. with all the worthiness and none of the shame. the madness of this moment and the litany of my future failures will all be okay.*

*space. in drawing, is 70% of what i think about. now at least. not always. it's my subject. the space of the paper. the space of the drawing in the room. the spaces within the drawing. i am after all, drawing space. space that feels like a thing. oh, that's a deep room. or a shallow pool. or a profile. or i'm above or beneath. part of what i love is that none of it is real. not in a drawn world. when people get hung up on the representational elements in my work, i can't help but to laugh a little. have i tricked you? are you impressed by the fact that flat shape looks like a three-dimensional human? i laugh because i'm not impressed at all. i find it quite unspecial in fact. and to draw a line or to render a form is all the same to me. none of it is anything. i'm just playing around.*

*i imagined you must be a dancer. former? can one ever stop such a thing? maybe you no longer perform? but you dance still. i know it. thanks for saying i'm not an imposter. that felt sincere. and i trust you. no, i'm not an imposter. i have a right to move my body in such a way that brings me joy. or opens a portal. or makes me remember my elbow. we forget so much about this package we're living inside of. can you breathe with me? take a deep breath. feel your stomach expand, your shoulders drop. exhale. i was reminding myself as i was writing. i was in that bad habit of breathing from my throat. so inadequate. so lazy. now i want to stand up and explore something else . . . i tried your comment. about direct and elusive. illusive. allusive. they all confuse me and i mean some of each. i tried it in my living last week. it was hard and fun. thank you for the prompt!*

*you asked about creativity. i agree with you . . . that it's not about being an artist necessarily. i think it's a way of thinking. a curiousity or something about problem solving . . . being innovative. i think in any field/profession/human being, creativity can exist. and does. until it doesn't anymore. until we are taught away from it. suppressed. i don't have any more monopoly or access than the next person. i am just connected to it and welcome it in my life. i'm not afraid of it. maybe the failure is the fear? well, i'm not afraid of that either. so i try stuff. haha . . . like making a dance company! the artist kerry james marshall said inspiration is generated by work. when i first heard this, i held on tight. yes! at last! it's not magic. it's as tangible as anything else if you do it. or let it know it's okay . . . it's welcome. have you heard elizabeth gilbert's ted talk on the creative genius?*

*so i wrote this: I don't think of my body as mine necessarily*

*and you wrote: I could concretely feel the distance between my-self and my-flesh*

*we are on the same page! . . . dancing and running? i haven't thought about that. the first thought that popped into my mind was: the ability to fly. now, drawing and running is something i've thought about. Gaia, they are the same thing! analogue expressions/languages. simple and slow (one foot in front of the other. meters accumulating to miles and miles and miles). inner traversing through an outward gesture. a deeply spiritual, meditative practice. gentle. violent. unassuming in their potency. there was a stretch when i was boxing. i'd leave the studio and go meet my trainer. that felt like a departure. an opposite action. but to go from drawing to running was one in the same. i continued these sweeping movements. gliding across paper and concrete. thinking the entire time. and also, zoning out.*

*i'm going to pause here for now as it's late on my end.*

*for now, goodnight. speak soon.*

---

*i'm back. how is your day going?*

*narrative. i used to say i was a storyteller, but now i'm not so sure. or i mean, i am—of course—we all are. but i have a better sense of the ways that are natural for me/my body to tell a story. i've always described the work as non-linear. that felt right. still does. i add to that now, non-narrative. which we both know, still means narrative, but a specific kind. i liken it to a subgenre of film. or dance, even. when you can feel a story, but don't know. where you are given open pieces, elements, enough to grasp perhaps—but not too much so all your questions are answered. i'm not interested in that type of narrative. beginning middle end. susie went to the store and met billy they went for ice-cream it was cold the end. before the pandemic i would go to the cinema by myself. i love to be alone. i'd usually go to the first show at 10:30, sometimes 11. I'd sneak in a pork bun from the asian bakery next door and milk tea. and i'd sit with the other three people in the theater (usually over the age of 60) and watch my movie in peace. i like the foggy kind of stories. i like when time is sliced and rearranged. i like stories about strangers or pseudo lovers. connections that overlap but are mostly unknown. i like the visceral quality of a story. the sense of beauty. pure beauty. and a little darkness. or maybe the mundane. i like a little boredom in my story.*

*yes, hard to escape the narrative. impossible perhaps. human beings. we're wired to find it, to crave it, to invent it. i don't resist this at all. i think i am more resistant to single sided story telling. one directional. hierarchal perhaps? the storyteller knows. and they impart the story onto the listener. where is the responsibility of the listener? or the see-er? can't we mold this thing together? after all, once there is an audience, there are so many additional points of view, histories, contexts, favorite things to eat for breakfast, astrological signs all mixing together. i remember a grad professor who refused to interact with my piece. she said, she didn't want to have to do anything for art. i disagree. yeah, maybe i won't pull you onto the dance floor, but you will do something. you will exist. and i must acknowledge the power of that. and how it changes everything. you mentioned independence in the viewer. absolutely. i'm not there anymore. in the art, i mean. i did something and then i left. now it's yours. you hold it. or not. but it's no longer mine.*

*also maybe you can answer a dance question for me . . . well, i guess it ties into your comment/question about disciplines. and the borders between them. i think they're getting more and more arbitrary and i like that, i suppose. or i get it. it is the era of the interdisciplinary. which in some ways, leaves me out in the cold. i'm so fucking stubborn about drawing. i must draw. and no, i will not use a computer or put it on canvas and also say i'm a writer and an activist and an artist. i only say two things. artist who draws. and runner. so i'm not cool like the new kids who do all the things. and i'm committed. monogamous to my medium. and that matters to me. the allegiance. it just worked out that way, i didn't do it on purpose. i want to be aligned with this thing—drawing. i am very intentionally placing myself in its path and being consumed by all that it is. dance, as you know is a new public expression for me. i might call it drawing, still. but my question . . . how come dance doesn't have to explain itself? or does it and i just don't know? visual artists will still get that horrible question: what does it mean? are dancers exempt? or are people needing each movement to be accountable to a story that you must share? you must tell the audience everything you ever thought?!! people demand that from visual art, particularly by artists of color—Black and brown specifically. we're supposed to explain ourselves. it is a freedom to not have to say anything at all. to let the work be. i am trying more and more.*

*I bid you adieu.*

This correspondence between ruby onyinyechi amanze and Gaia Clotilde Chernetich started in March 2021 in order to shed light on the choreographic and performative features of amanze's artworks. The exchange of letters allowed the conversation to evolve spontaneously and to create a concreter connection in these times where distance and separation decline all human activities. Correspondence let distance, and the impossibility of meeting, to become an empowered characteristic of this encounter, and not an obstacle.

Gaia Clotilde Chernetich is a former dancer currently working as a dramaturg and dance scholar based in Italy.

# "E POI C'È QUALCOSA CHE RIGUARDA LA BELLEZZA". UNA CORRISPONDENZA CON RUBY ONYINYECHI AMANZE

Gaia Clotilde Chernetich

Questo testo è nato da un esercizio d'immaginazione e da una proposta. Ho chiesto a ruby onyinyechi amanze di iniziare una corrispondenza. Ora lo considero uno scambio fondato su una sincerità reciproca e affettuosa. Inaspettata. Abbiamo usato la lettera come strumento rivelatore, ci siamo tuffate e abbiamo danzato. Adesso è il momento di trasmettere questi pensieri ai nostri futuri lettori.

12.03.21

Cara Ruby,

dopo la videochiamata in cui abbiamo deciso di iniziare questa corrispondenza, ho cercato di ricordare che cosa ho provato l'ultima volta che ho visitato la Collezione Maramotti. È stato qualche mese prima che scoppiasse la pandemia. Mi ha stupito sapere che eravamo entrambe presenti alla performance site-specific di Dimitris Papaioannou. Prima ancora di conoscerci, abbiamo condiviso un'esperienza che ha creato un riferimento spazio-temporale comune. Ricordo il silenzio e la luminosità particolare dello spazio. Quel pomeriggio la luce era color pastello. Ho visitato le gallerie. Ero impaziente di vedere la performance. La presenza della danza e della performance art negli spazi espositivi solleva tantissime domande. Ho letto che pratichi danza e del tuo interesse per la performance, potresti dirmi qualcosa di più?

Quando mi capita di chiedermi "quanto siamo liberi" noi esseri umani in questo momento, non ho risposte. Sento che le restrizioni che stiamo vivendo hanno il potere di cambiare la percezione che abbiamo di noi stessi; di sicuro hanno questo potere su di me. Personalmente trovo libertà nella parte più "ristretta" di me stessa, il mio corpo. Sembra un ossimoro, lo so. Ma, se oggi esiste una qualche forma di libertà, per me può essere soltanto una forma di resistenza. Non saprei dire se si tratti di una sorta di resilienza. È possibile vivere in questo "nuovo habitat" e creare arte senza riferimenti al nostro passato recente (e, a quanto pare, già perduto)? Diventeremo un nuovo tipo di generazione fondata sulla memoria e dipendente dal passato? Ci troviamo in uno stato di "sospensione", in attesa di poter creare un nuovo rapporto con il nostro corpo e con il nostro passato/presente/futuro?

La situazione attuale legata al coronavirus sottolinea la centralità del nostro corpo. So che nella tua ricerca artistica è presente l'elemento corporeo. Penso per esempio ai tuffatori e danzatori che disegni. La tua prospettiva sul corpo è cambiata con la pandemia? Come coinvolgi il tuo corpo nella tua pratica artistica? È un punto di partenza o una sorta di "luogo" in cui sviluppi qualcosa che è emerso prima, mentre stavi disegnando?

Vedo per noi la possibilità di diventare una generazione che deve misurarsi con costanti riferimenti a esperienze passate, vissute e archiviate in un arco di spazio e di tempo che è svanito all'improvviso… Non so se questi concetti trovano riscontro in te e nel tuo lavoro, ma siccome io stessa sono parte della "generazione successiva" di una comunità della diaspora (nel 1947 la mia famiglia ha abbandonato la sua terra natale, l'Istria, da profughi), vedo molti legami tra il presente che stiamo vivendo e un nuovo capitolo di potenziali traumi.

Prenditi cura di te, cara Ruby

Gaia

17.03.21

*carissima Gaia, voglio dire carissima, perché anche se non ti conosco – questa è intimità. quello che stiamo facendo. il modo in cui condividiamo qualcosa. mi piace che sia così e non a senso unico o autoritario. mi è sembrato giusto già il giorno in cui ti ho parlato durante quella videochiamata. lavorare a questa cosa insieme. e affrontarla di lato anziché di fronte. sotto alcuni aspetti sono diretta. stabile come il mio segno zodiacale [scorpione]. molto chiara e precisa su ciò che provo e su come voglio che siano le cose. ma perlopiù fluttuo. sono oscura. e sono elusiva. è la mia natura. tu come ti muovi? cosa si potrebbe dire della tua essenza?*

*e forse questa è una domanda troppo semplice, ma sei una danzatrice?*

*il corpo. ne hai parlato. le limitazioni al movimento… al tatto… alla vicinanza. sì, avverto tutte queste cose. uno dei legami più duraturi, e a questo punto più concreti, con il mio corpo è quello della macchina. ho corso a livello agonistico per oltre 2 decenni. lo farei ancora, se la corsa fosse consentita. non considero il mio corpo come necessariamente mio. cioè, ovviamente lo è. ma io lo incarno. sono un alieno. e ho scelto di abitarlo per poter esperire il mondo. è necessario per alcune cose, per esempio correre. saltare nelle pozzanghere. mangiare del cibo e capire se a te (chi sei tu?) piacciono determinati sapori. ho allenato il mio corpo. gli ho parlato come se fosse un io separato. corpo, per favore, fai questa cosa. grazie, corpo.*

*lo uso anche per disegnare. disegnare è come correre. voglio continuare a dirlo – continuare a parlarne –, ma mi sembra che la gente non ascolti davvero.*

*non credo che questo per me sia cambiato. con la pandemia, voglio dire. e no, non voglio che sia al centro di questa conversazione. non so cos'altro si possa dire, mentre la si vive. dopo, forse? mi chiedo come sarà il futuro, tra cinque anni. questa cosa che è successa. per me è stata discreta. non mi ha colpita in modo catastrofico. anche la discrezione è pericolosa però. sì, le mie molecole si sono spostate, ma non so quale sia la portata del cambiamento. forse sono un po' insensibile. troppo vicina alla normalità per avere le parole giuste per descrivere... questa cosa. mi mancano tutto e tutti. ecco cosa dico nei giorni più tristi. gli altri giorni sono __________. per quanto riguarda l'arte, l'arte sopravvive a qualsiasi cosa, no? anche la performance. so che è stata colpita più duramente degli altri medium. o che la "svolta" è stata più visibile, più necessaria. alcune cose non si possono tradurre allo stesso modo, però. il digitale non può respirare come noi. i bulbi oculari sulla carne emettono un'energia che lo schermo di un computer non può emettere. aspetti che passi o usi quest'altra versione? e se quest'altra versione va in un certo senso contro il tuo centro?*

*è buffo che abbiamo condiviso lo stesso spazio alla Collezione Maramotti. eravamo l'una di fianco all'altra? ai capi opposti della sala? mi hai vista? io probabilmente ti ho vista. esamino a fondo le stanze piene di gente. voglio scoprire ogni segreto.*

*mi piace quello che hai scritto sulle generazioni. e sull'essere figlia della diaspora. lo sono anch'io – non sono una discendente di profughi, ma sono un'immigrata. quindi una parte di me capisce cosa voglia dire trovarsi in una terra altra. non ho mai capito come funzionino davvero le generazioni. ho una figlia. ma credo che ci separino due generazioni. non dovrebbe essere una sola? penso che tu abbia ragione... ci avvicineremo al futuro con un ricordo attivo del passato. l'anno scorso tante persone non hanno festeggiato il compleanno – non che i compleanni siano indicatori attendibili della realtà, ma è pur vero che quell'anno è svanito nel nulla. è scomparso dalla faccia della terra. non è pervenuto. ma è stato ricordato nel nostro sangue. ho parlato troppo della cosa di cui non voglio parlare? forse. possiamo istituire un divieto, adesso? ci siamo liberate entrambe di un peso...*

*quali domande solleva la danza nei musei? è una questione di pubblico? di vicinanza? è considerata problematica? tutto è problematico. ricordo il periodo del judson dance theater a new york. forse non è esatto dire che lo ricordo, perché all'epoca non ero ancora nata, però sento che siamo allineati. tutti quei discorsi sugli spazi e sulle gallerie e sulla danza come arte figurativa e i tentativi di abbattere le barriere e arrivare alla gente in modi più "autentici". la mia amica wura non sopporta che le gallerie spingano in tutti i modi i loro artisti a fare una performance per le inaugurazioni. come se i visitatori delle gallerie dovessero essere intrattenuti, come se l'arte visiva non bastasse. o come se la performance fosse uno spettacolo che va consumato passivamente, come la televisione. nessuna di queste cose è vera.*

*amo l'architettura e gli spazi della Collezione Maramotti sono fantastici! non so ancora dove si svolgerà la nostra danza. ci realizziamo in una sorta di vuoto. in uno spazio fra più mondi. quando arriviamo dobbiamo distruggere tutto. mettere tutto a nudo. vedere che aria si respira nelle sale. a Reggio Emilia. funzionerà bene? dobbiamo imparare a conoscerla [la danza] e a conoscere noi stessi partendo quasi da zero. si trasformerà in una nuova creatura. non si può prendere qualcosa e metterlo in un posto diverso e aspettarsi che resti identico.*

*nei miei disegni traccio a inchiostro le piscine e prendo qualcosa in prestito dalla pittura. continuo a disegnare, in parte, per via del medium. per quanto mi piacerebbe oppormi ["odio" la pittura e non ho remore in merito], non posso fingere di non essere pittorica in quei momenti. e a dire la verità adoro che il mio punto d'accesso sia caratterizzato dall'ignoranza. o dall'ingenuità. so essere sincera come un bambino. nuova. esplorativa. pervasa dalla gioia e dalla goffaggine. dall'imperfezione. c'è troppa pressione rispetto alla maestria. la danza non fa eccezione. ossa che si contorcono in forme che in teoria sarebbero più adatte a fare una cosa che forse i corpi non dovrebbero fare. e che dire di tutti i momenti prima di quello in cui il corpo trasmette il movimento al cervello? e che dire delle ossa troppo grandi o squadrate, quando invece dovrebbero essere arrotondate? e se si volesse restare immersi nella curiosità e nell'umiltà del non sapere? ancora per un po'. perché dico tutto questo? stavo pensando alla danza. e a me. e al fatto che non ho una preparazione classica. il mio compagno non fa che chiedermi se sono un impostore. come posso accettare il fatto che ora sono una danzatrice. "all'improvviso". sembra peggio di quello che è. mi piace essere sfidata...*

*non è all'improvviso, però. è da sempre. ballo da sempre. e negli ultimi cinque anni ho passato molto tempo a pensare, guardare, leggere, disegnare, respirare la danza. mi mancano un sacco di cose. non conservo il vigore nei muscoli, così come non conservo la pittura e mai lo farò.*

*non nego la realtà e voglio poterne parlare. avvicinarmi a tutto questo. capire dove può portarmi/permettermi di andare. quali porte posso aprire da qui? insieme a Mor, che conserva il ricordo. l'accumulo di storie, allenamenti, contesto, lingua.*

*ho fatto delle performance, in passato. perlopiù cose dalla texture traballante. o solenni e fondate sulla resistenza. nelle opere performative – molto spesso sono un corpo per un altro artista. raramente sono un mio concetto/progetto. mi piace muovermi e danzare. conosci il linguaggio di movimento gaga? era fonte di grande felicità quando vivevo a new york. adoro esplorare l'aspetto tattile dello spazio. è di questo che parlano i miei disegni, alla fine. deriva dalla condizione di immigrata, ma quello è solo l'inizio della storia. ormai è una storia vecchia. forse persino irrilevante... ma nasce dagli spostamenti e dall'utilizzare pezzi di terra o ricordi per creare nuovi pezzi di terra o ricordi. il vuoto tra mondi diversi. la divisione dell'io in tutti i luoghi in cui è stato il corpo. le sovrapposizioni e il modo in cui il cielo si curva. il modo in cui l'acqua trasforma i segreti.*

*e poi c'è qualcosa che riguarda la bellezza.*

*quella è l'altra parte del movimento, per me. la grazia. la delicatezza del tracciare una linea con il dito.*

*e ovviamente cos'è la bellezza senza fisicità? forza bruta. resistenza. un'assoluta assenza di grazia.*

*mi sembra di avere tantissimo da dire ma di averne detta solo una piccolissima parte. mi capisci? dico cose sensate? come proseguiamo?*

*grazie per avermi scritto. vorrei che fosse tutto analogico. ho un debole per carta e penna.*

22.03.21

Carissima Ruby,

fuori dalla mia finestra Roma è deserta, la gente non esegue nessuna coreografia per strada: tutti camminiamo, ci spostiamo, condividiamo sempre meno. O, meglio, possiamo condividere, ma separatamente. Oggi comunque c'è il sole e l'aria è fresca, quasi *primaverile*. Sono andata al parco con mio figlio. La città sembra anestetizzata. Di nuovo. Finirà presto, dicono.

In questo contesto generale di separazione/separazioni, scriverti – comunicare con te negli USA, dall'altra parte dell'oceano – e parlare di qualcosa di tuo che si svolge, a livello fisico, più vicino a me che a te...

crea una strana percezione dello spazio. Spazio è una delle parole chiave di questo periodo. Pensi allo spazio, quando disegni o prepari qualcosa da esporre? Sono una dramaturg di danza (sono – stata – una danzatrice, sì!), e lo spazio è un aspetto con cui mi confronto molto.

Come consideri la creatività? Coinvolge direttamente la danza nei tuoi lavori? Poco tempo fa ho parlato con un amico del concetto di "essere creativi". Per me, l'"essere creativi" non è qualcosa che va necessariamente di pari passo con l'essere artista.

Mi ha colpito che tu abbia scritto: "Non considero il mio corpo come necessariamente mio". È la *forma mentis* di un danzatore! Ho vissuto in questo modo. Non perché sia mai stata spossessata del mio corpo, ma perché, per *essere* una danzatrice, ho lasciato entrare i pensieri degli altri così a fondo dentro di me che, a volte, sentivo concretamente la distanza tra *me-stessa* e la *me-stessa-corpo*. Trovi che ci sia un legame tra il tuo interesse per la danza e l'essere una runner? Disegnare è come correre, hai scritto.

C'è una storia particolare che vuoi esprimere o raccontare attraverso la tua arte? E, se sì, che tipo di medium è il tuo corpo? Come danzatrice, ma anche come dramaturg di danza e autrice, penso sia impossibile evitare la narrazione. Può non essere nei tuoi intenti o nei tuoi occhi, ma quelli degli spettatori sono fatti per rendere le cose comprensibili attraverso la vista, innanzitutto. Da questa prospettiva, poiché i nostri occhi hanno dei superpoteri (ci portano dentro le immagini, no?), come coinvolgi gli spettatori nelle tue opere?

Non sei un impostore quando danzi. Nessuno può essere un impostore quando muove il proprio corpo. La performance è ovunque. Sono curiosa di sapere cosa pensi dei confini tra le varie discipline. Artisti visivi, performance artist, artivist, ecc. Dal mio punto di vista, tutte queste categorie si stanno fondendo e confondendo tra loro. E, allo stesso tempo, l'autoposizionamento è uno dei temi più importanti dell'ambito artistico.

Danza e musei o performance e gallerie sono binomi molto comuni. L'eterna domanda è: in che modo si influenzano a vicenda? È stato scritto molto in merito. Quale sarà la posta in gioco, in futuro?

Vorrei tanto che potessimo bere un caffè e proseguire questa conversazione faccia a faccia… e, anche se potrei continuare a scrivere, ancora e ancora, ora mi costringo a fermarmi e a cliccare su invia.

Grazie, Ruby.

Prenditi cura di te,

Gaia

01.04.21

*hai un figlio anche tu! mi ha fatto sorridere. un altro umano sconosciuto in società con un altro umano adulto che in qualche modo – in qualsiasi forma o maniera – si ritrova con una piccola creatura umana. proprio come me. proprio come miliardi di persone prima di noi e dopo di noi. sì, dalla prospettiva di un piccoletto è uno strano modo di interagire/ non interagire. ma sono più intelligenti di tutti noi. e nei primi mesi sulla terra le cose si cancellano. o vengono assorbite o si disintegrano in minuscoli, infinitesimali frammenti. anche per noi. stiamo già scorporando il ricordo che stiamo vivendo. dimentichiamo in tempo reale. mascherine? quali mascherine? due anni di vita si restringeranno. immagino che, con il passare di ogni anno, diventerà sempre meno reale. e due mesi di vita svaniranno del tutto. ma che ne sappiamo davvero? magari sono stati quei primi due mesi di vita a contare più degli altri. a renderci le persone che siamo. sono pronta a sbagliare tutto, da genitore. in tanti modi, pieni d'amore. ma la parte che farò bene sarà tracciare le sue basi – le sue fondamenta – il suo terreno iniziale – con tutto l'amore di cui sono capace. con tutte le conferme di cui io stessa ho bisogno. con tutta la stima e nessuna vergogna. la follia di questo momento e il lamento dei miei fallimenti futuri andranno bene.*

*lo spazio. quando disegno, è il 70% di ciò a cui penso. ora, almeno. non sempre. è il mio soggetto. lo spazio sulla carta. lo spazio del disegno nella stanza. gli spazi all'interno del disegno. in fondo sto disegnando spazio. spazio che sembra qualcosa. oh, è una stanza profonda. o una piscina bassa. o un profilo. oppure mi trovo al di sopra o al di sotto. tra le cose che amo c'è il fatto che nulla di tutto ciò sia reale. non in un mondo disegnato. quando la gente si fissa sugli elementi figurativi delle mie opere, non riesco a trattenere una risata. vi ho ingannati? vi colpisce che una forma piatta somigli a un essere umano tridimensionale? rido perché io non sono affatto colpita. in realtà mi sembra molto poco speciale. e disegnare una linea o creare una forma per me è la stessa cosa. nulla di tutto ciò significa qualcosa. sto solo giocando.*

*immaginavo che fossi una danzatrice. in che senso lo sei stata? si può smettere di esserlo? forse non ti esibisci più? ma balli lo stesso. lo so. grazie per aver detto che non sono un impostore. mi è sembrato sincero. e mi fido di te. no, non sono un impostore. ho il diritto di muovere il mio corpo in un modo che mi trasmetta gioia. che apra un portale. che mi faccia ricordare il mio gomito. dimentichiamo tantissime cose del pacchetto in cui viviamo. puoi respirare con me? fai un respiro profondo. senti lo stomaco che si espande, le spalle che si abbassano. espira. lo stavo ricordando a me stessa mentre scrivevo. stavo respirando dalla gola, una brutta abitudine. molto fuori luogo. molto pigro. ora voglio alzarmi e analizzare qualcos'altro… ho provato con il tuo consiglio. sull'essere diretta ed elusiva. illusiva. allusiva. queste parole mi confondono tutte, e intendo un po' di ognuna. l'ho provato in soggiorno la settimana scorsa. è stato difficile e divertente. grazie per il suggerimento!*

*mi chiedi della creatività. sono d'accordo con te… non riguarda necessariamente l'essere artisti. credo sia un modo di pensare. una sorta di curiosità o qualcosa che riguarda la risoluzione dei problemi… l'essere innovativi. credo che la creatività possa esistere in qualsiasi ambito/professione/essere umano. ed è così. finché non esiste più. finché non ci viene insegnato ad allontanarcene. a reprimerla. non ho più monopolio o accesso di nessun altro. sono soltanto legata a essa e la accolgo nella mia vita. non mi fa paura. forse il fallimento mi fa paura? be', non mi fa paura nemmeno quello. quindi provo cose diverse. ahah… come fondare una compagnia di danza. l'artista kerry james marshall ha detto che l'ispirazione è generata dal lavoro. quando l'ho sentito per la prima volta quasi non ci credevo. sì! finalmente! non è magia. è tangibile come qualsiasi altra cosa, se la fai. o se le fai sapere che va bene… che è la benvenuta. hai sentito il ted talk di elizabeth gilbert sul genio creativo?*

*e così ho scritto: non considero il mio corpo come necessariamente mio*

*e tu hai scritto: sentivo concretamente la distanza tra me stessa e la mia stessa carne*

*siamo sulla stessa lunghezza d'onda…! danzare e correre? non ci avevo pensato. il primo pensiero che mi è venuto in mente è stato: la capacità di volare. ho riflettuto sul disegno e sulla corsa. Gaia, sono la stessa cosa! espressioni/linguaggi analoghi. semplici e lenti (un piede davanti all'altro. metri che si sommano per diventare miglia e miglia e miglia). una traversata interiore grazie a un gesto verso l'esterno. una pratica profondamente spirituale e meditativa. delicata. violenta. senza pretese nella sua potenza. c'è stato uno strappo quando facevo boxe. uscivo dallo studio per vedermi con il mio allenatore. mi sembrava un punto di partenza. un gesto contrario. ma passare dal disegno alla corsa era la stessa cosa. continuavo a fare gli stessi movimenti ampi. scivolavo sulla carta e sul cemento. pensavo per tutto il tempo. ma mi estraniavo, anche.*

*ora faccio una pausa perché qui è tardi.*
*buonanotte, per ora. a presto.*

---

*rieccomi. come sta andando la tua giornata?*

*la narrazione. un tempo dicevo di essere una storyteller, ma ora non ne sono più tanto sicura. cioè, lo sono – ovviamente –, lo siamo tutti. ma ho una percezione migliore delle modalità di raccontare una storia che risultano più naturali per me/il mio corpo. ho sempre descritto il lavoro come non lineare. mi sembrava opportuno. mi sembra ancora opportuno. ora aggiungo anche non narrativo. che, lo sappiamo entrambe, significa comunque narrativo, ma di un tipo specifico. lo paragono a un sottogenere cinematografico. o alla danza, anche. quando percepisci una storia, ma non la conosci. quando ricevi pezzi, elementi aperti, quanto basta forse per cogliere il senso generale – ma non abbastanza da dare risposta a tutte le tue domande. quel tipo di narrazione non mi interessa. inizio metà fine. susie andò al supermercato e incontrò billy andarono a mangiare un gelato faceva freddo fine. prima della pandemia andavo al cinema da sola. mi piace stare da sola. di solito andavo al primo spettacolo, alle 10:30, a volte alle 11. mi portavo di nascosto un panino al maiale comprato alla panetteria asiatica lì di fianco e un tè al latte. e mi sedevo in sala con le altre tre persone presenti (di solito ultrasessantenni) e guardavo il film in pace. mi piacciono le storie un po' fumose. mi piace quando il tempo viene spezzettato e riorganizzato. mi piacciono le storie che parlano di sconosciuti o di pseudo amanti. collegamenti che si sovrappongono ma restano perlopiù ignoti. mi piace l'aspetto viscerale di una storia. il senso della bellezza. la bellezza pura. e un po' di oscurità. o forse la banalità. mi piacciono le storie un po' noiose.*

*sì, difficile sottrarsi alla narrazione. forse impossibile. esseri umani. siamo naturalmente portati a cercarla, a desiderarla, a inventarla. non mi oppongo affatto a tutto ciò. credo di oppormi di più a una narrazione unilaterale. unidirezionale. gerarchica, forse? lo storyteller lo sa. e impone la storia all'ascoltatore. dov'è la responsabilità dell'ascoltatore? o dello spettatore? non possiamo modellare insieme questa cosa? dopotutto, quando c'è un pubblico ci sono tantissimi punti di vista, storie e contesti diversi, cibi preferiti per la colazione, segni zodiacali che si mescolano tra loro. ricordo una professoressa dell'università che rifiutò di interagire con la mia opera. disse che non voleva dover fare nulla per l'arte. non sono d'accordo. okay, magari non ti trascino sulla pista da ballo, ma dovrai comunque fare qualcosa. esisterai. e io devo riconoscere il potere di questa cosa. il fatto che cambi tutto. hai parlato dell'indipendenza dello spettatore. assolutamente. io non ci sono più. nell'arte, intendo. ho fatto una cosa e poi me ne sono andata. ora è vostra. potete custodirla. oppure no. ma non è più mia.*

*tra l'altro forse puoi rispondere a una domanda sulla danza… be', immagino che si leghi al tuo commento/alla tua domanda sulle discipline. e ai confini che le separano. credo che stiano diventando sempre più arbitrari, e penso che mi piaccia. o comunque lo capisco. siamo nell'epoca dell'interdisciplinarietà. il che, da un certo punto di vista, mi esclude. sono dannatamente tenace circa il disegno. devo disegnare. e no, non userò un computer e non lo metterò su tela e non dirò che sono anche una scrittrice e un'attivista e un'artista. dico due cose soltanto. artista che disegna. e runner. quindi non sono cool come i nuovi arrivati sulla scena che fanno tutto. e sono devota. monogama rispetto al mio medium. e per me è importante. la fedeltà. è semplicemente andata così, non l'ho fatto apposta. volevo sentirmi allineata con questa cosa – il disegno. mi sto posizionando su questa strada, voglio che mi consumi in ogni suo aspetto, e lo faccio in modo decisamente intenzionale. la danza, come sai, è per me una nuova forma di espressione pubblica. potrei comunque definirla disegno. ma ecco la mia domanda… perché la danza non deve spiegarsi? o lo fa e io non lo so? gli artisti visivi continueranno a sentirsi porre quella domanda terribile: cosa significa? i danzatori ne sono esonerati? o la gente ha bisogno che ogni movimento sia riconducibile a una storia che dovete condividere? dovete dire al pubblico tutti i pensieri che avete mai formulato?!! la gente lo esige, dall'arte visiva, soprattutto dagli artisti di colore – specialmente quelli dalla pelle nera o marrone. ci si aspetta una spiegazione, da noi. non essere obbligati a non dire nulla è una forma di libertà. poter lasciare che l'opera sia e basta. ci provo sempre di più.*

*Ti dico adieu.*

Questo scambio di lettere fra ruby onyinyechi amanze e Gaia Clotilde Chernetich è iniziato a marzo 2021 allo scopo di illustrare gli aspetti coreografici e performativi delle opere d'arte di ruby. La corrispondenza ha permesso alla conversazione di evolversi in modo spontaneo e di creare un legame più concreto in un periodo in cui la distanza e la separazione influenzano ogni attività umana. La corrispondenza ha lasciato che la distanza, e l'impossibilità di incontrarsi, diventassero un punto di forza di questo incontro, anziché un ostacolo.

Gaia Clotilde Chernetich è un'ex danzatrice che attualmente lavora come dramaturg e studiosa di danza; vive in Italia.

# HOW TO BE ENOUGH

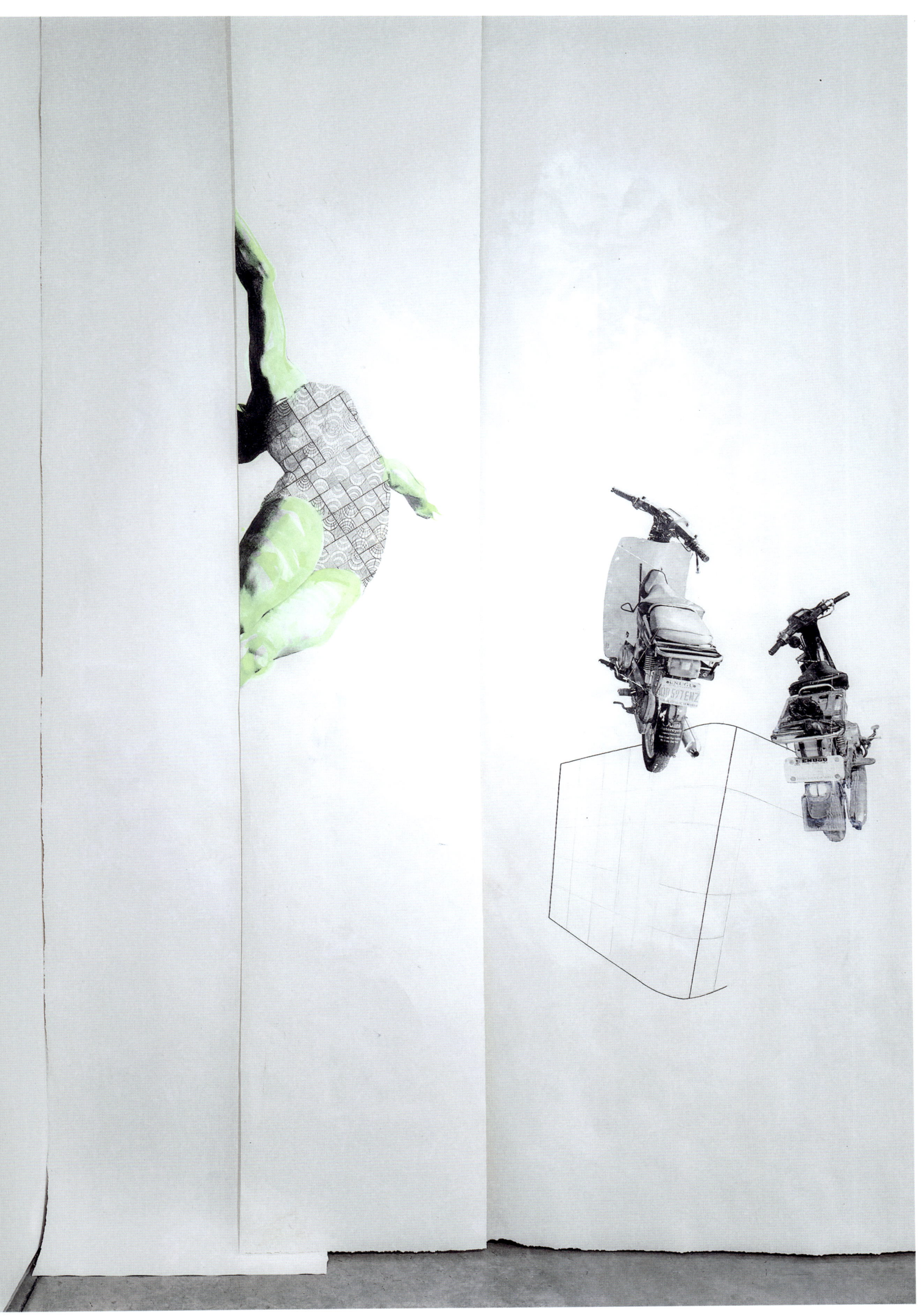
ENUGU
597ENZ
ENUGU

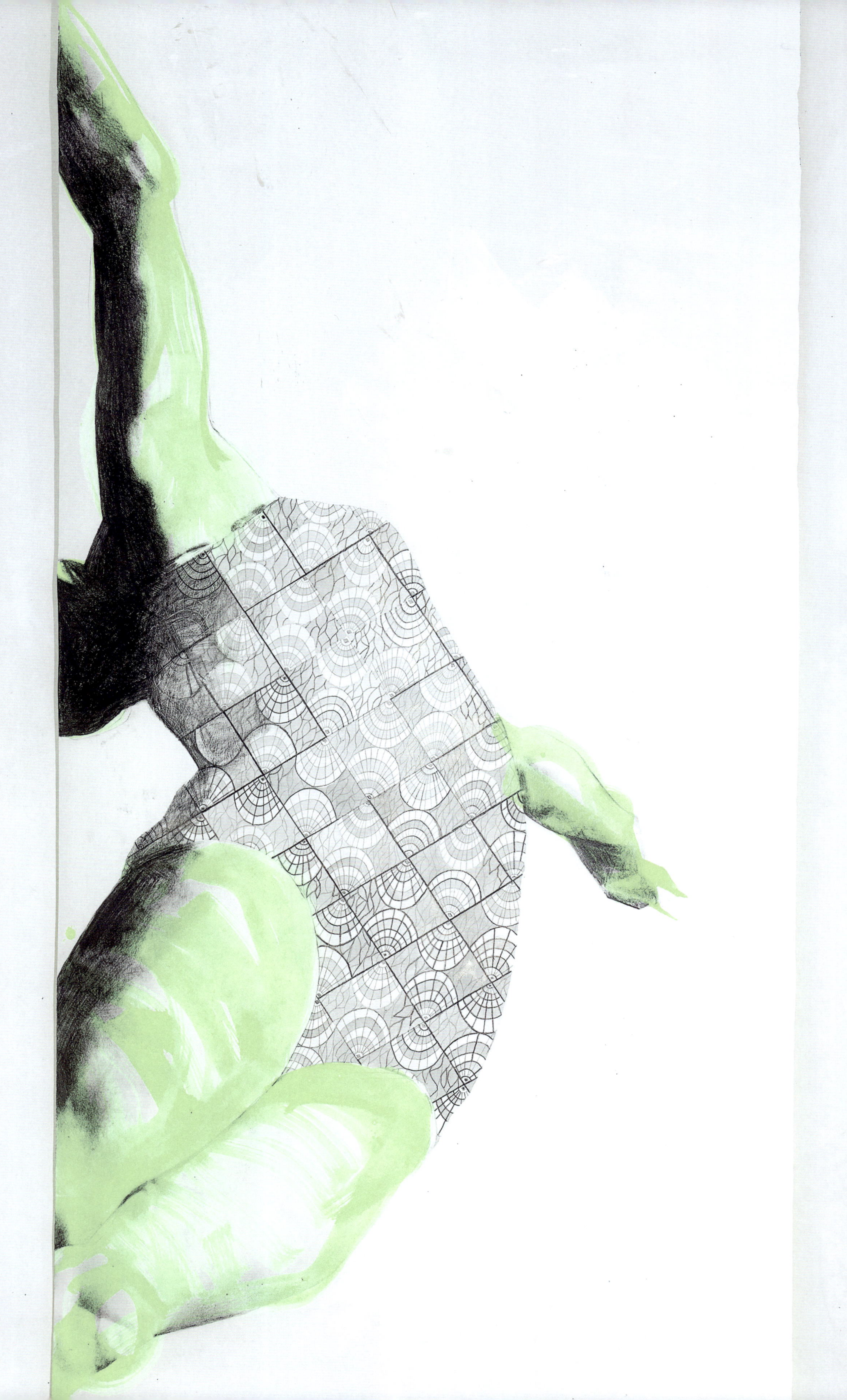

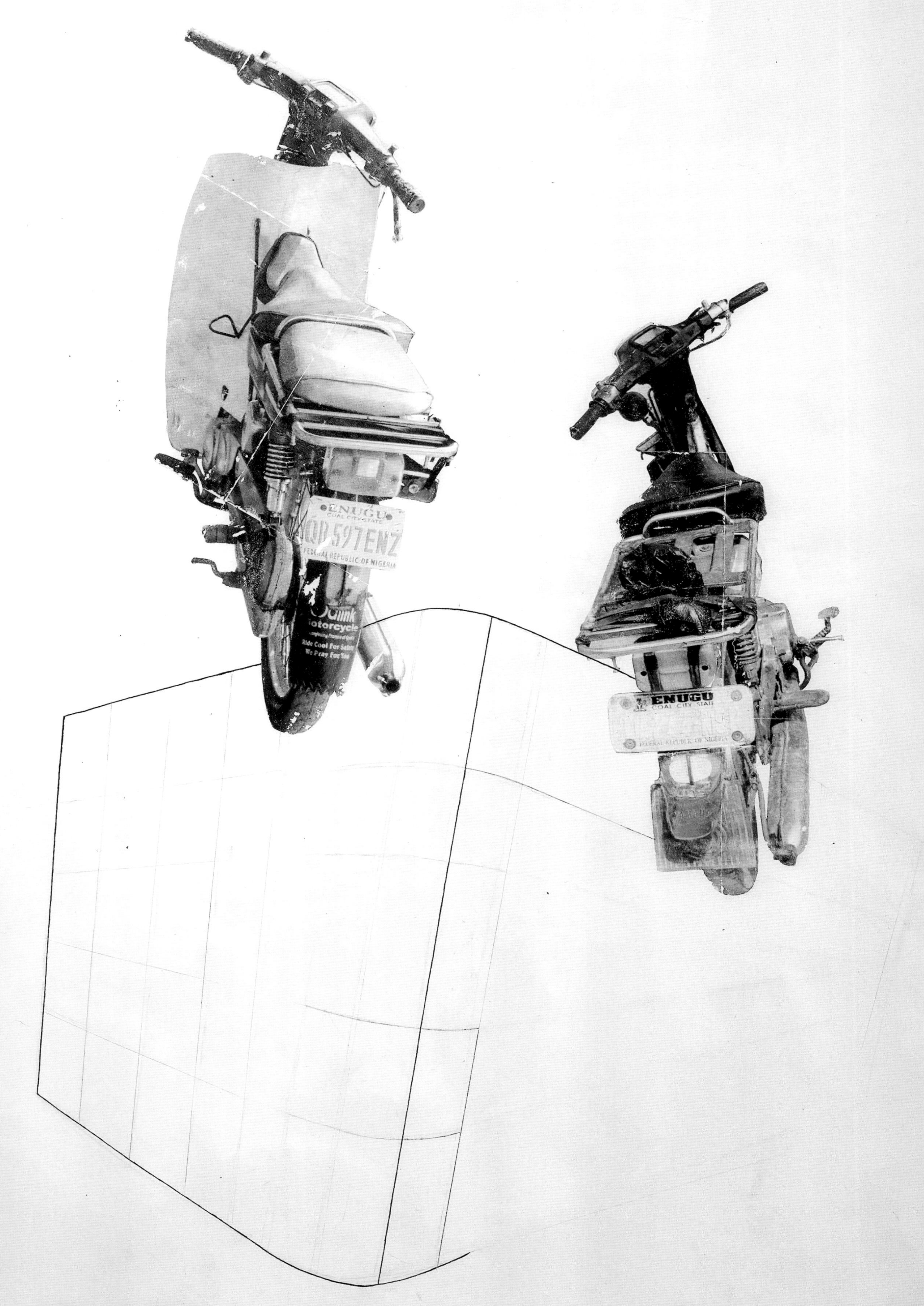
ENUGU
COAL CITY STATE
597ENZ
REPUBLIC OF NIGERIA
otorcycle
Ride Cool For
We Pray For You
ENUGU
COAL CITY

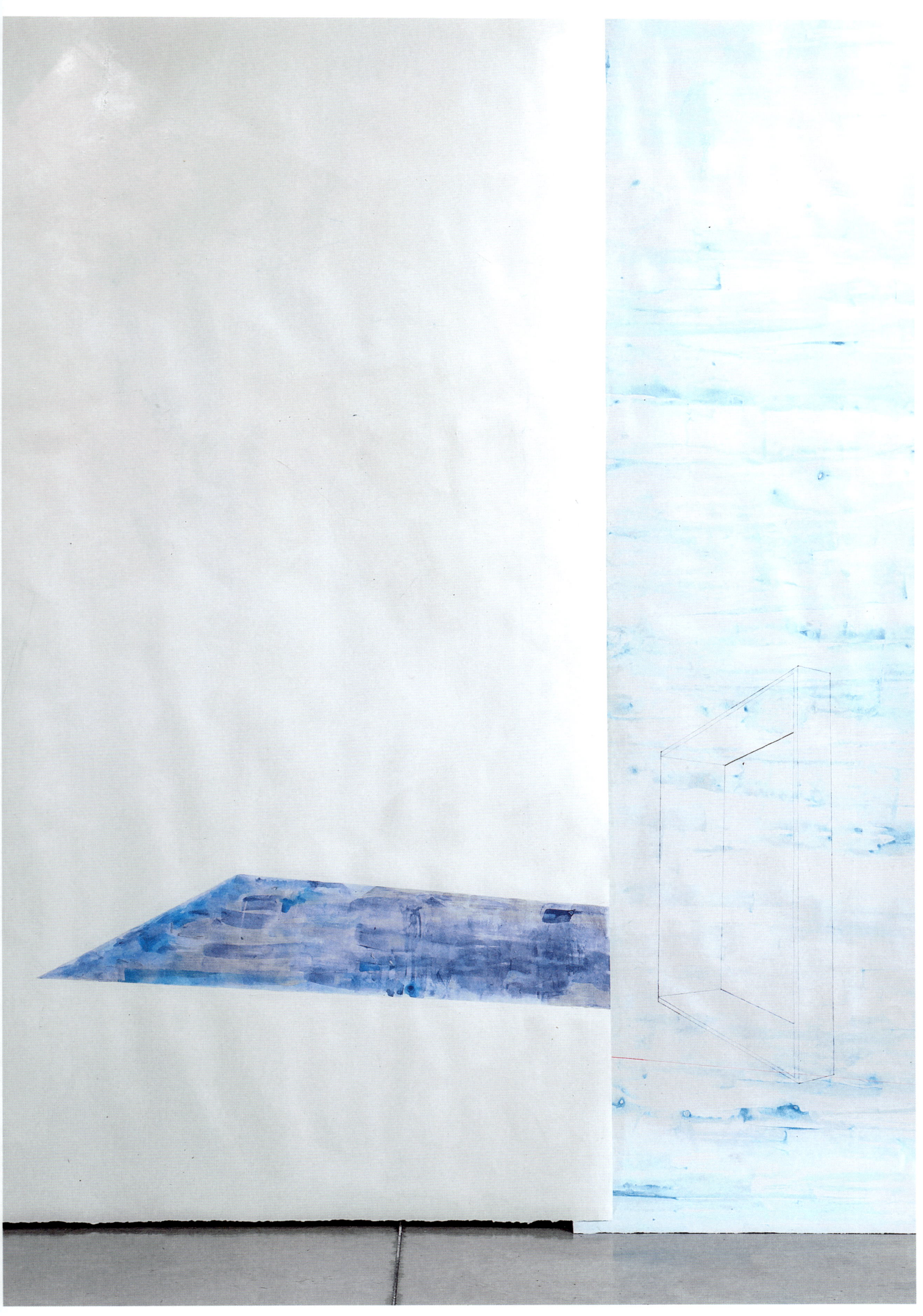

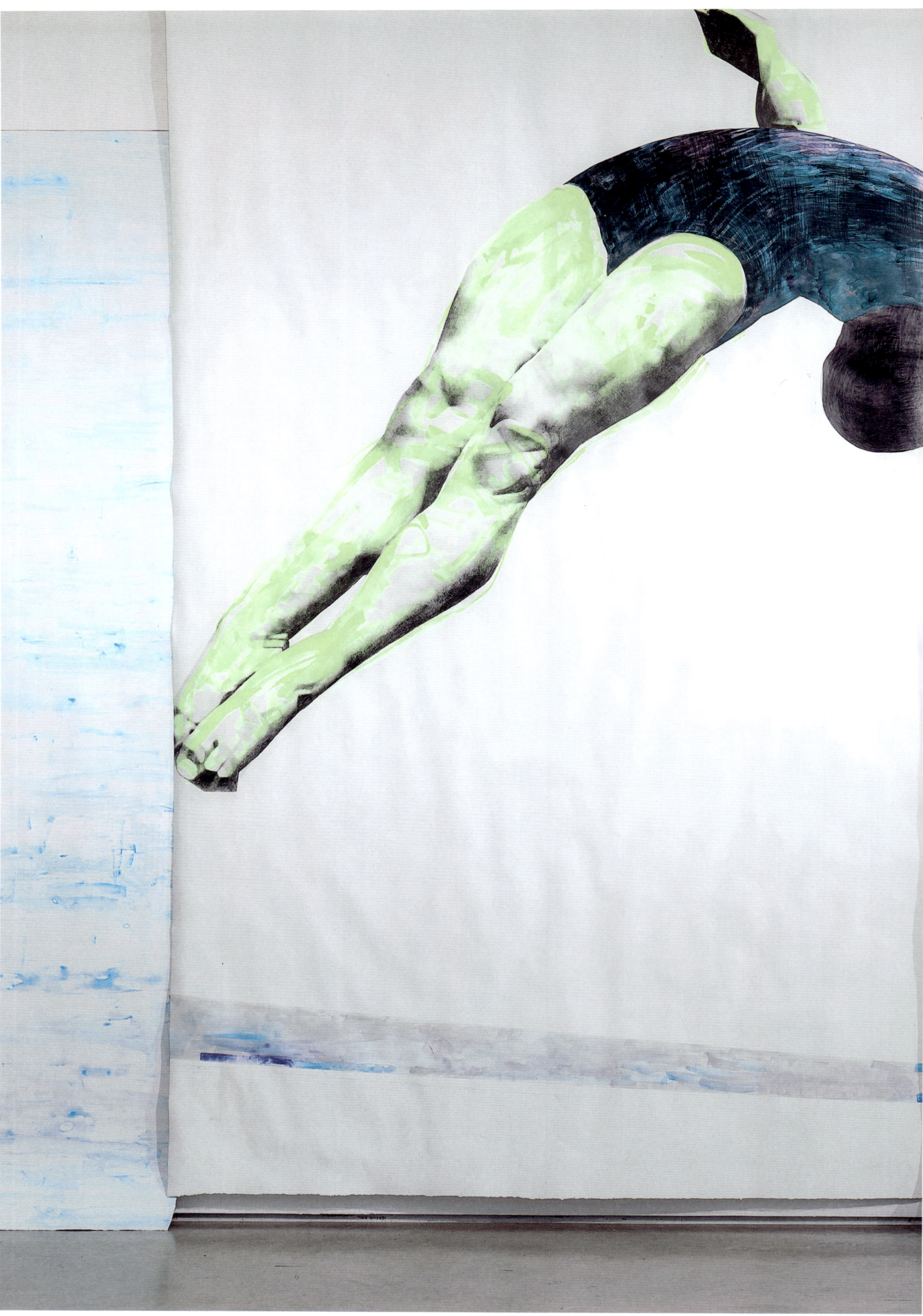

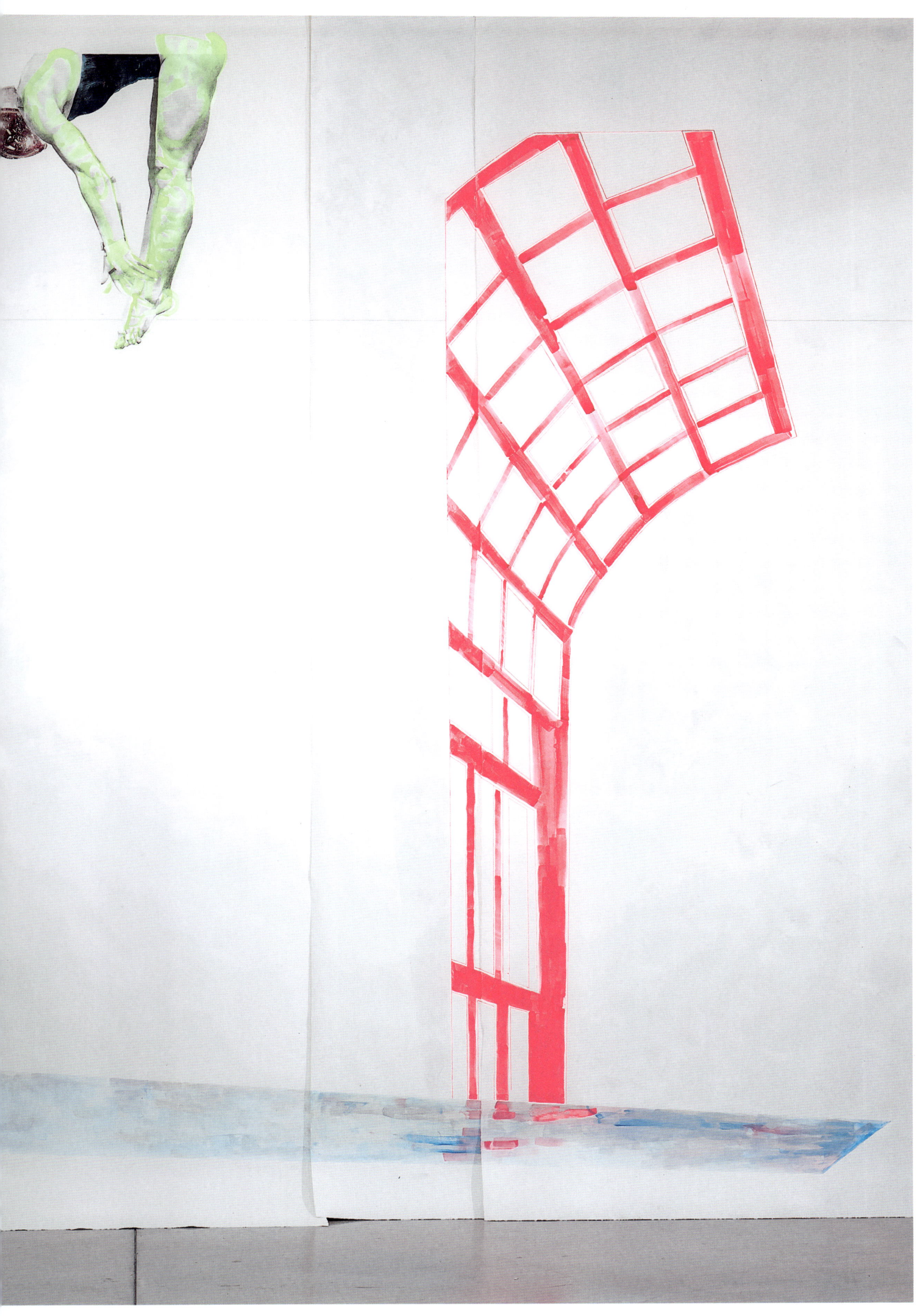

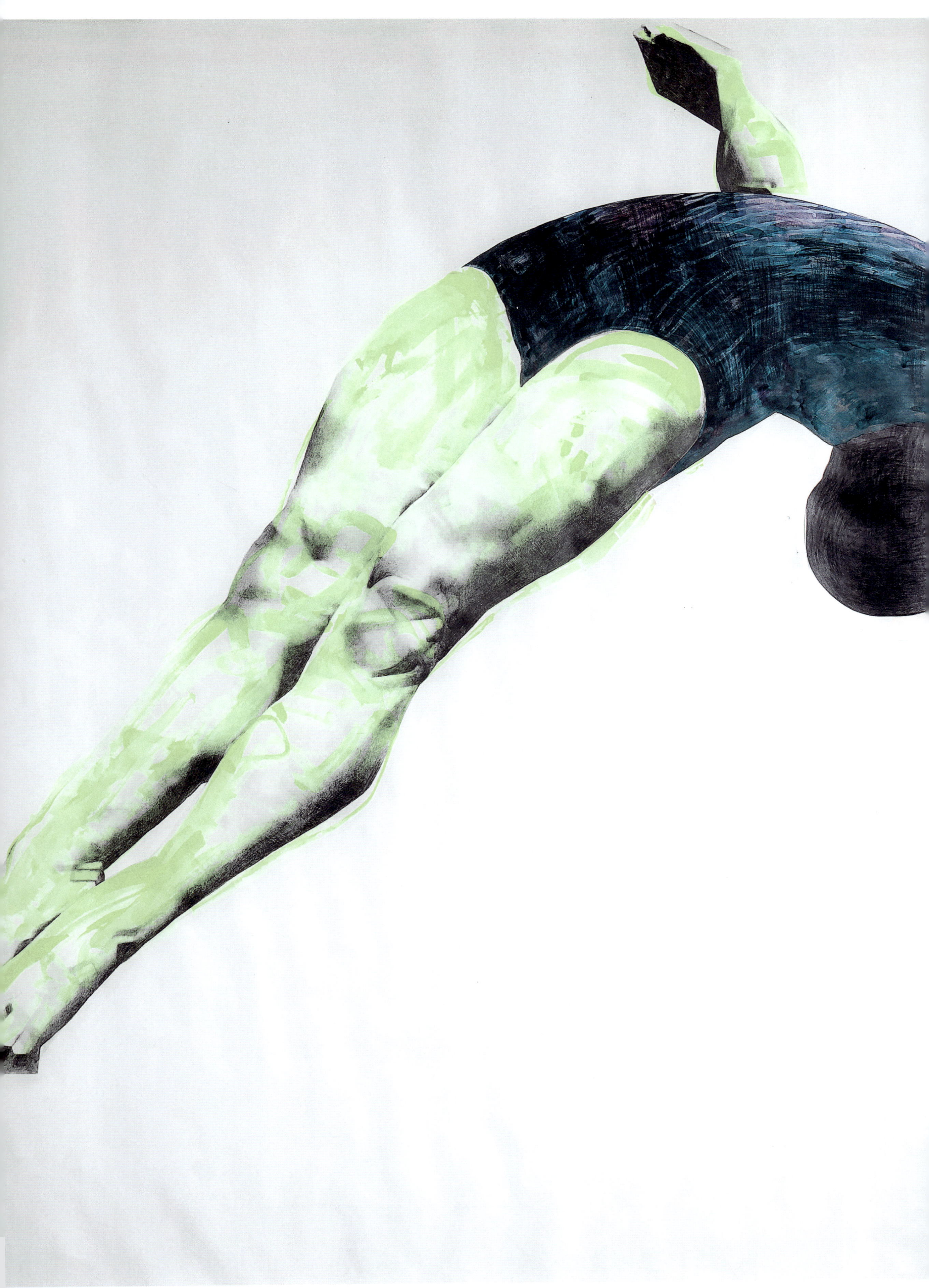

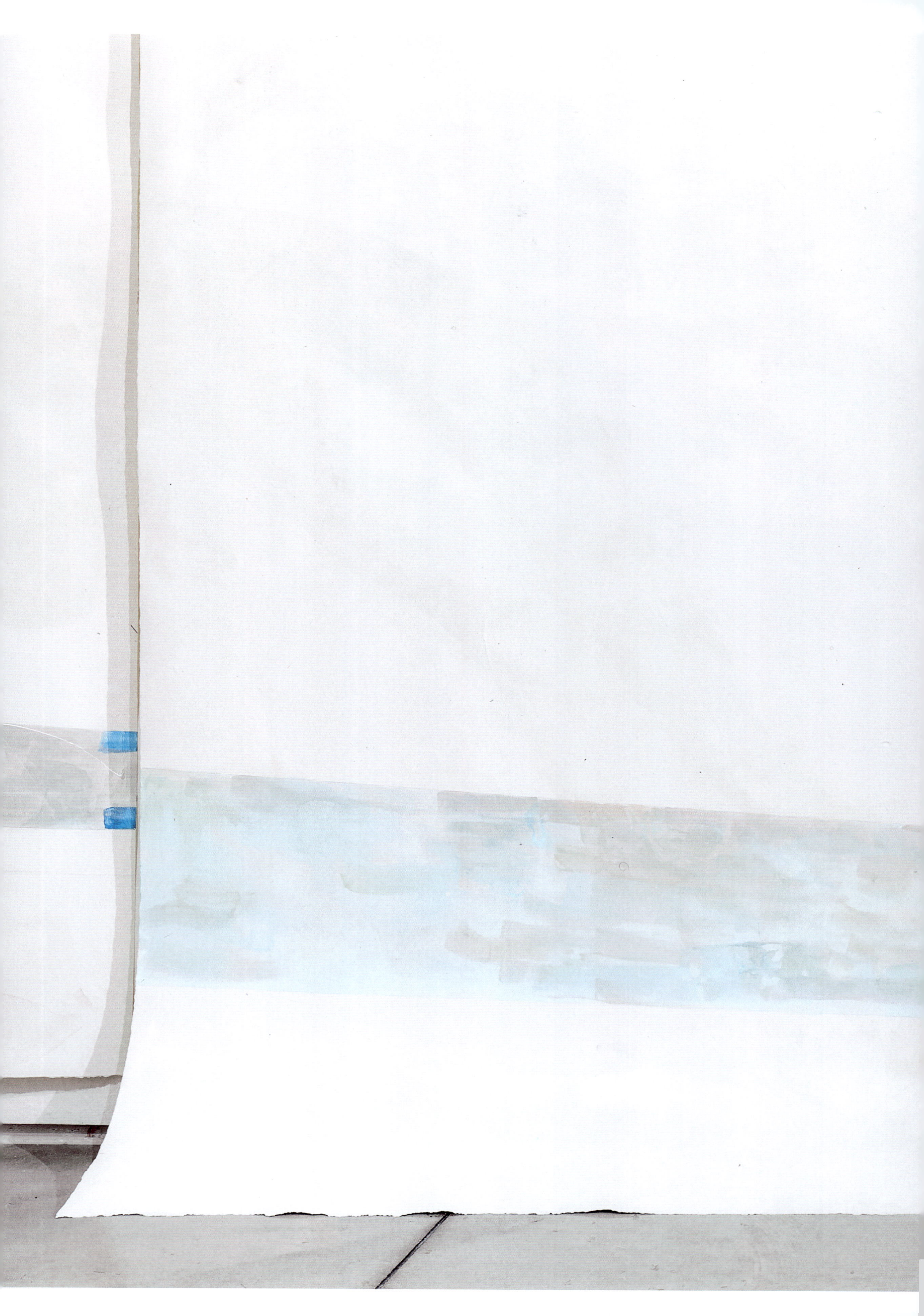

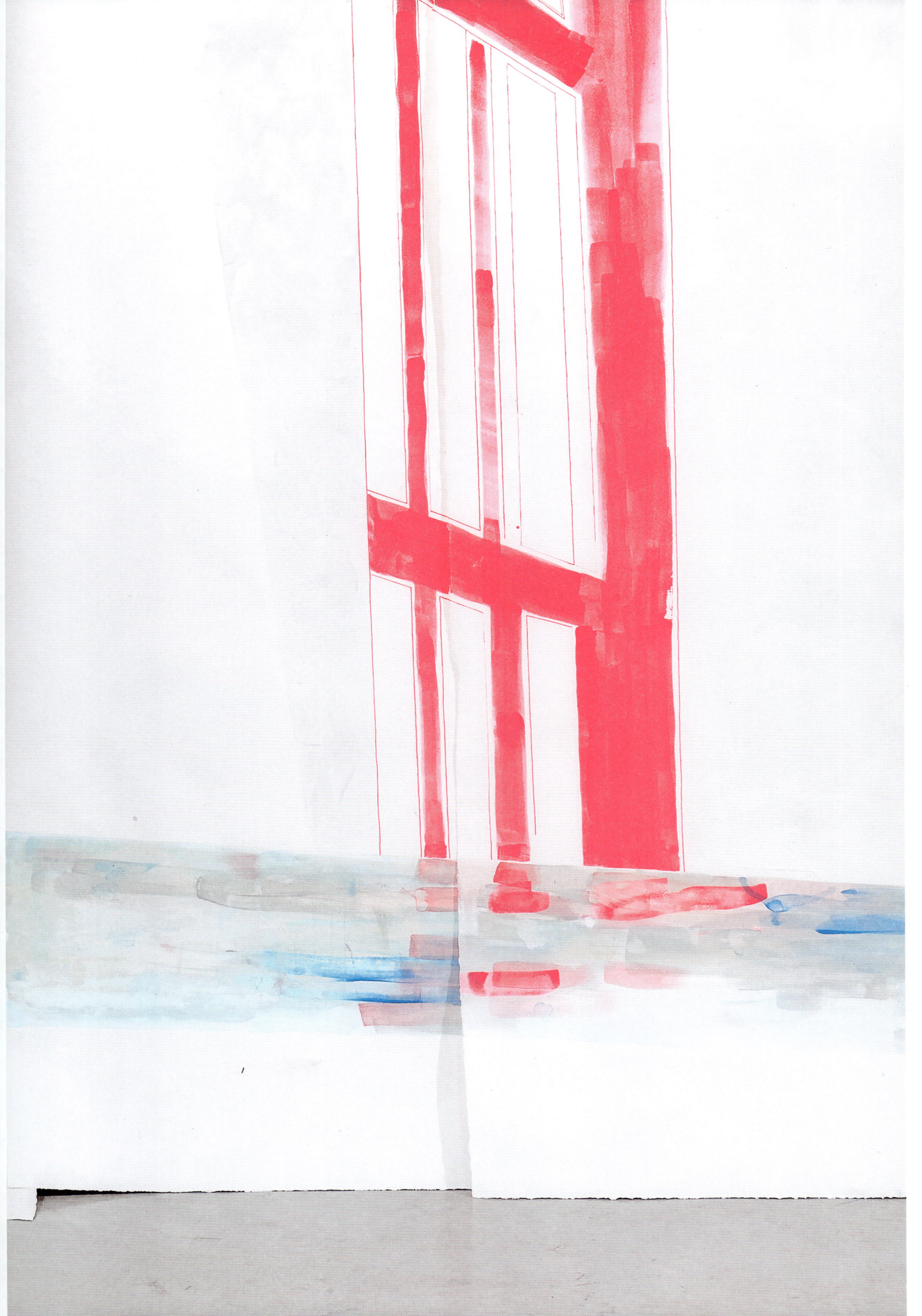

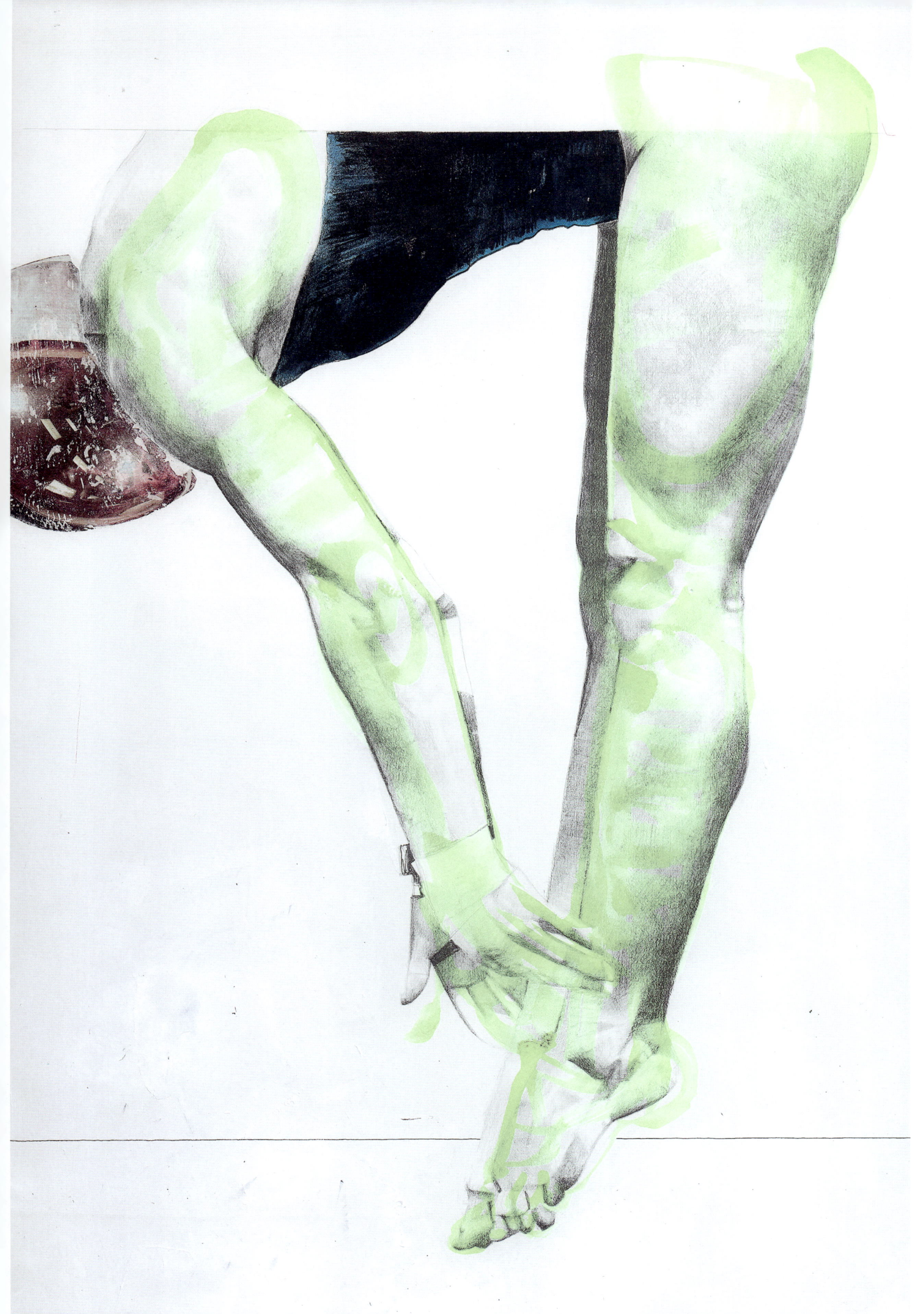

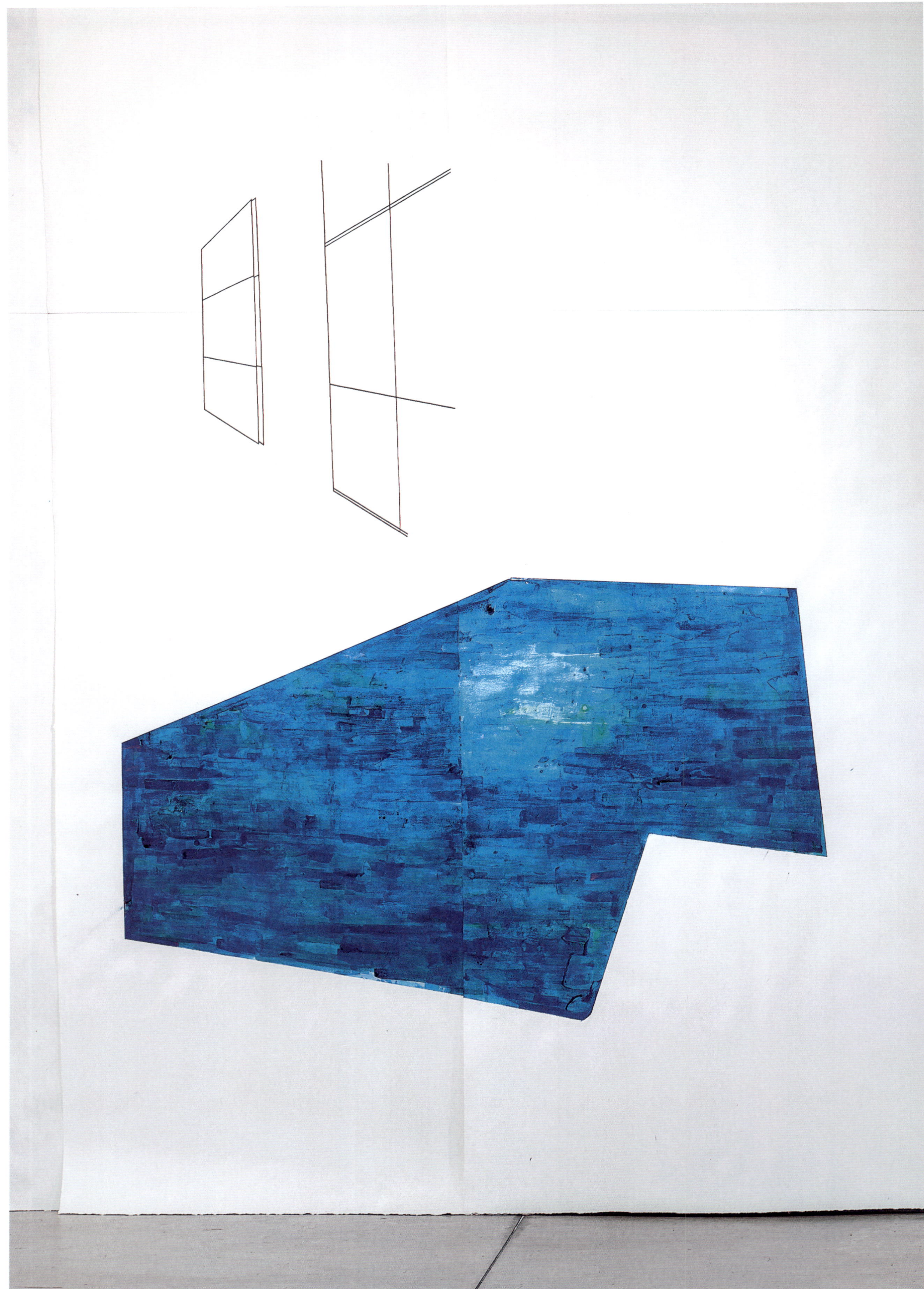

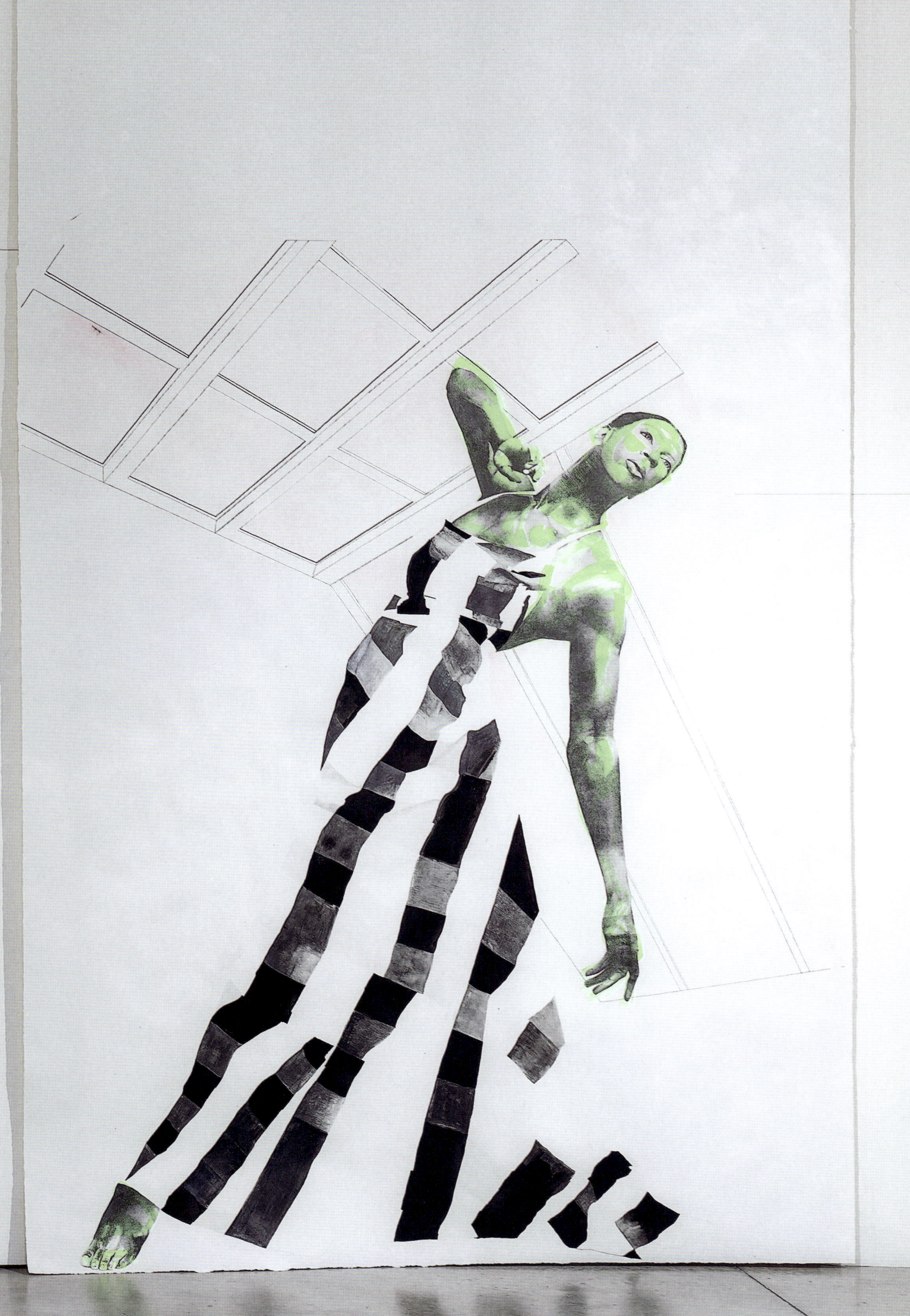

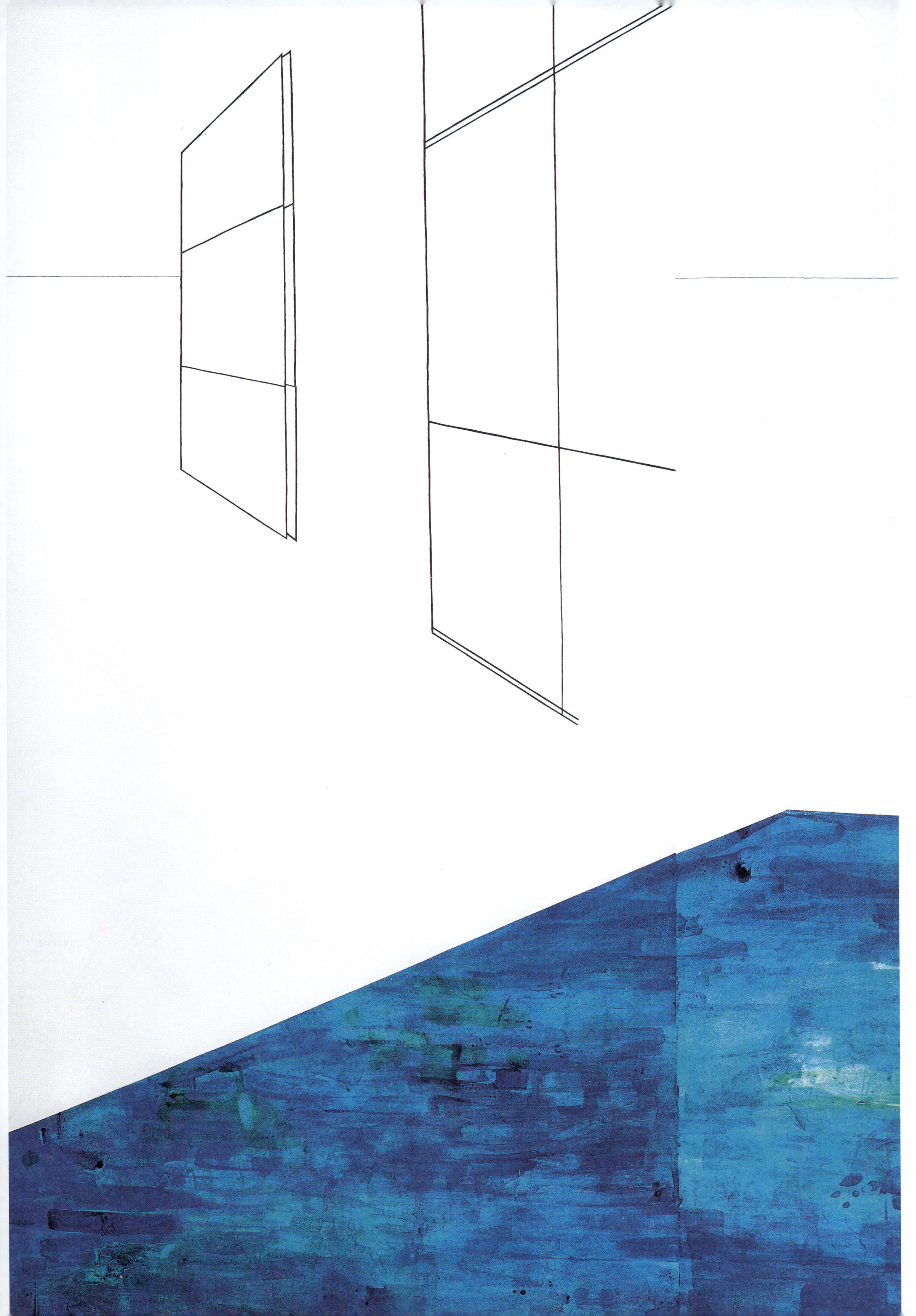

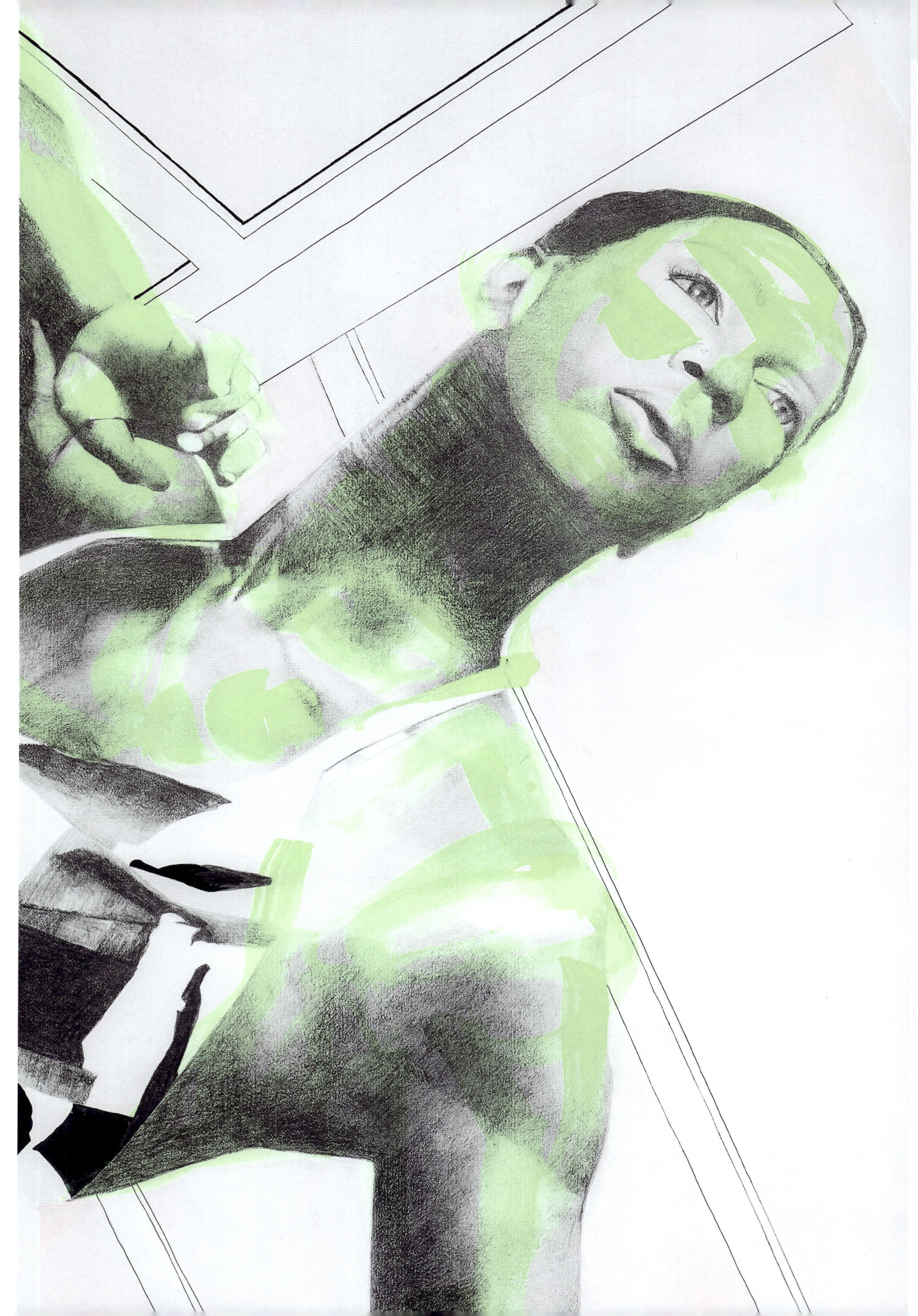

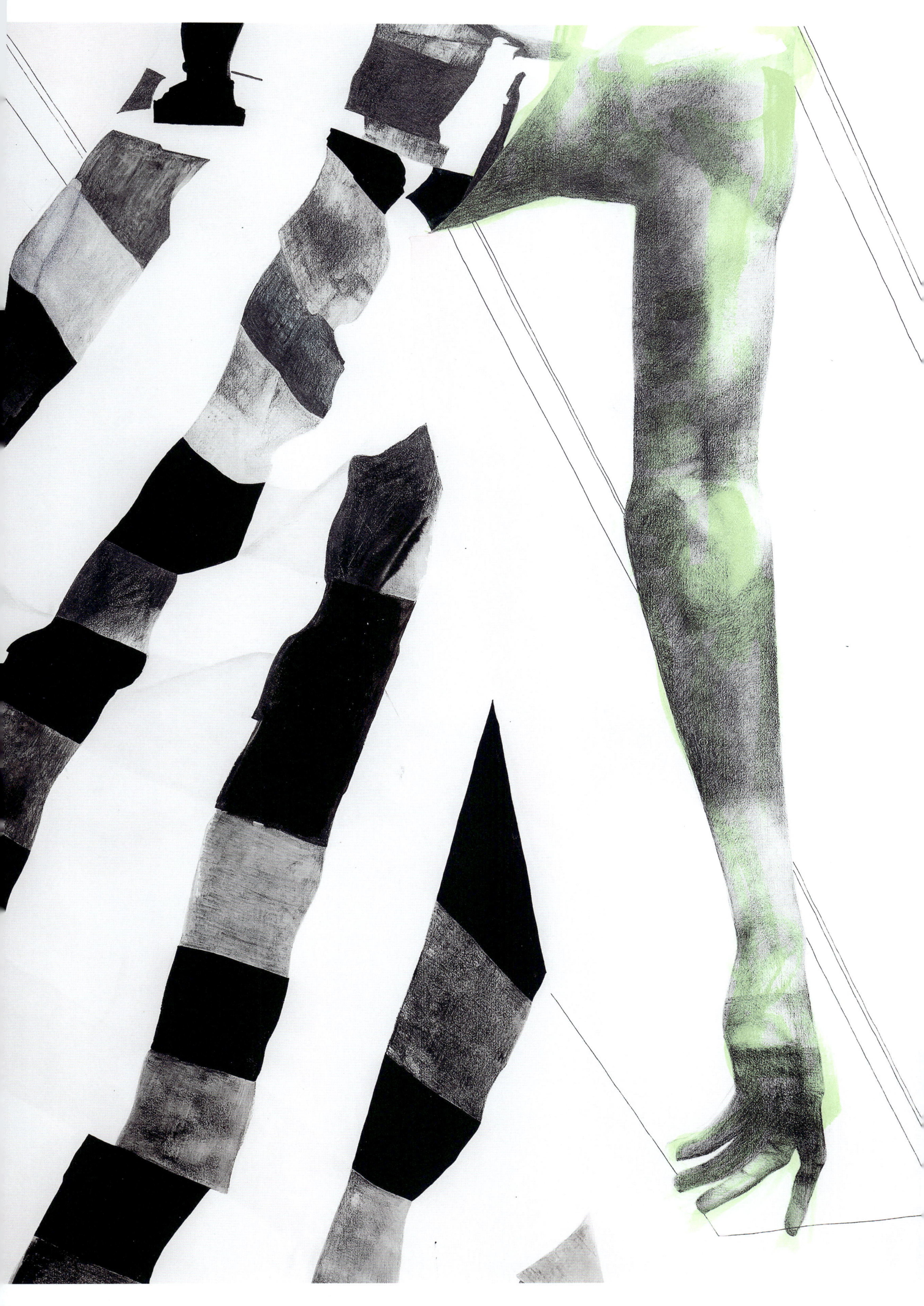

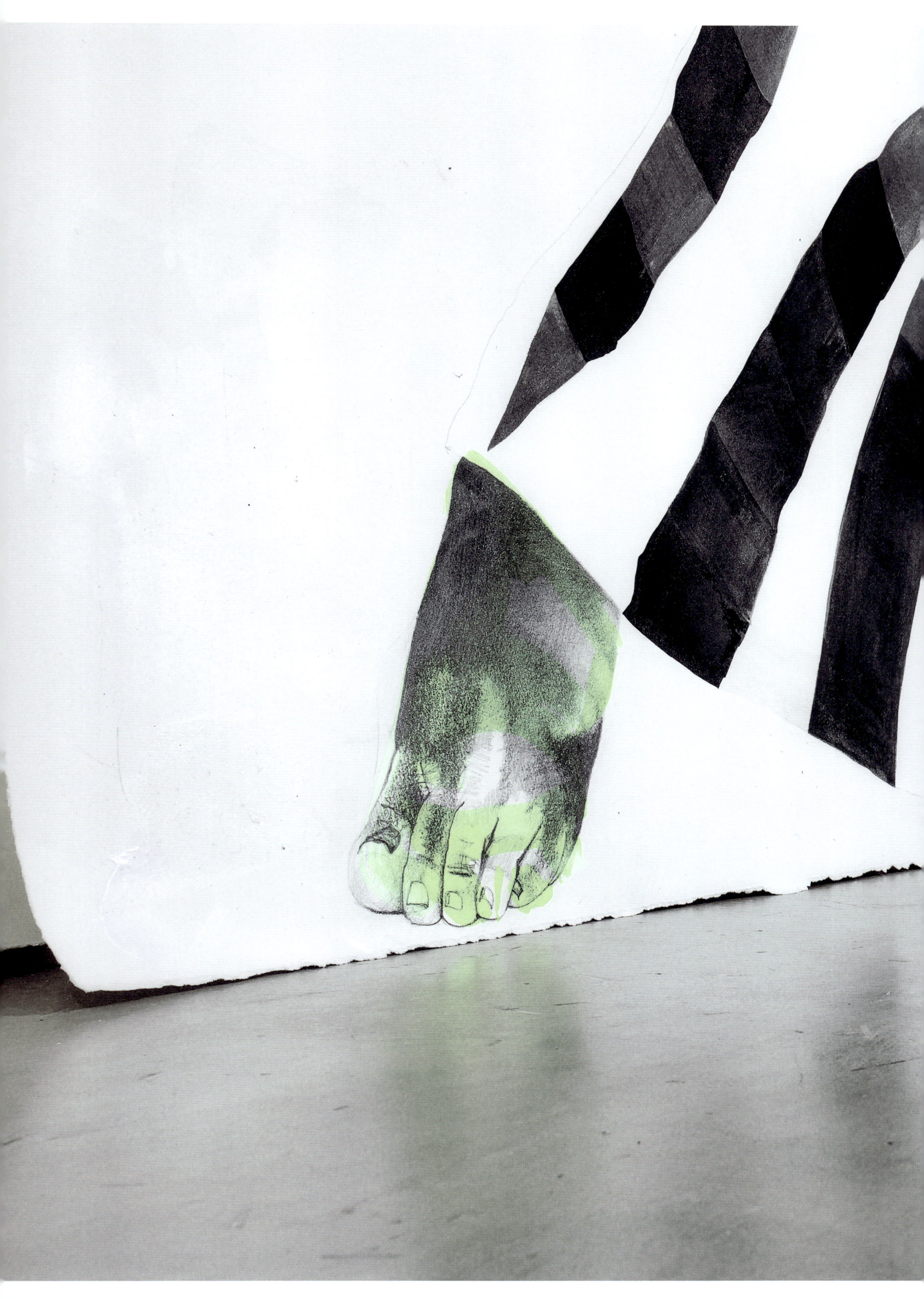

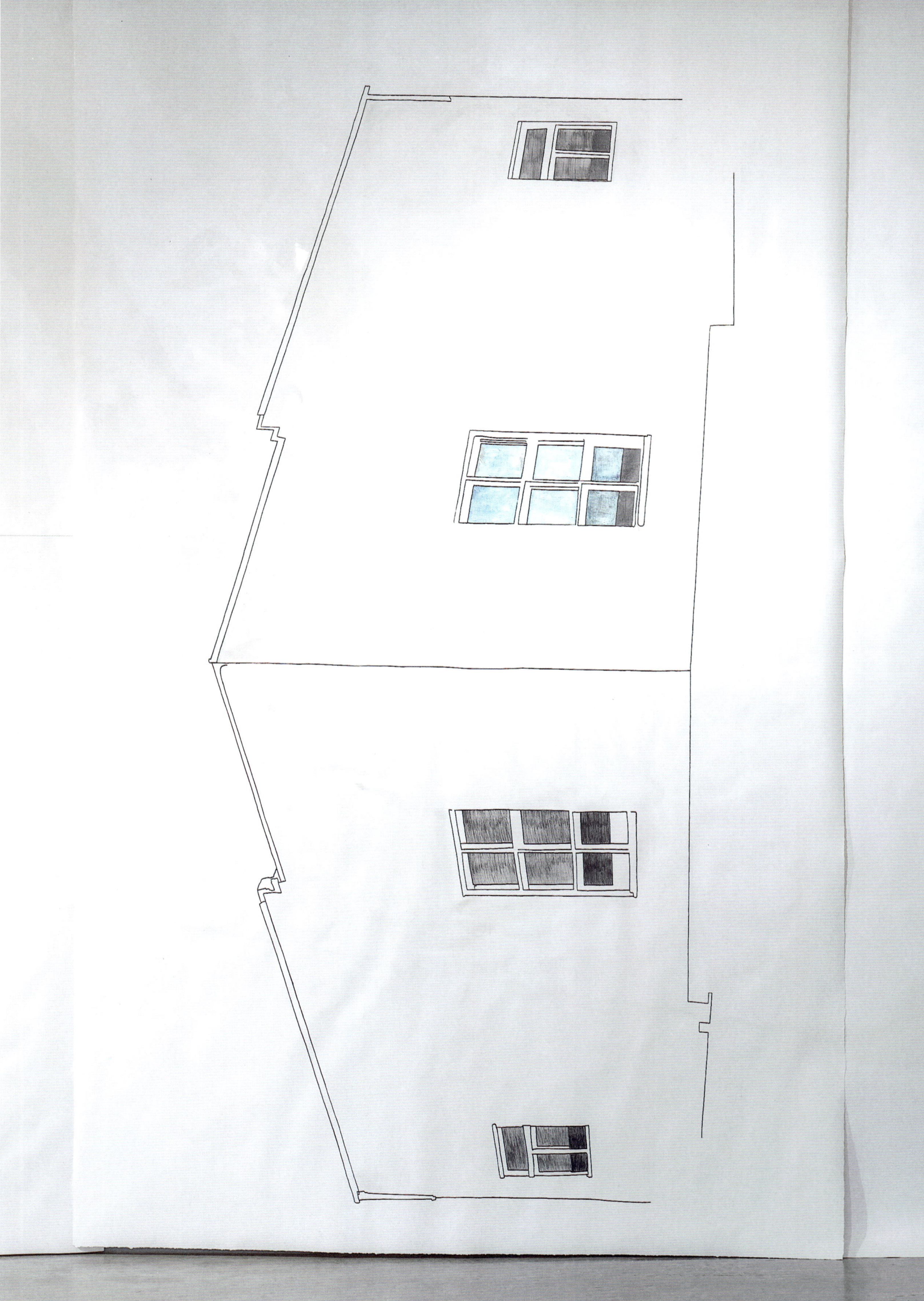

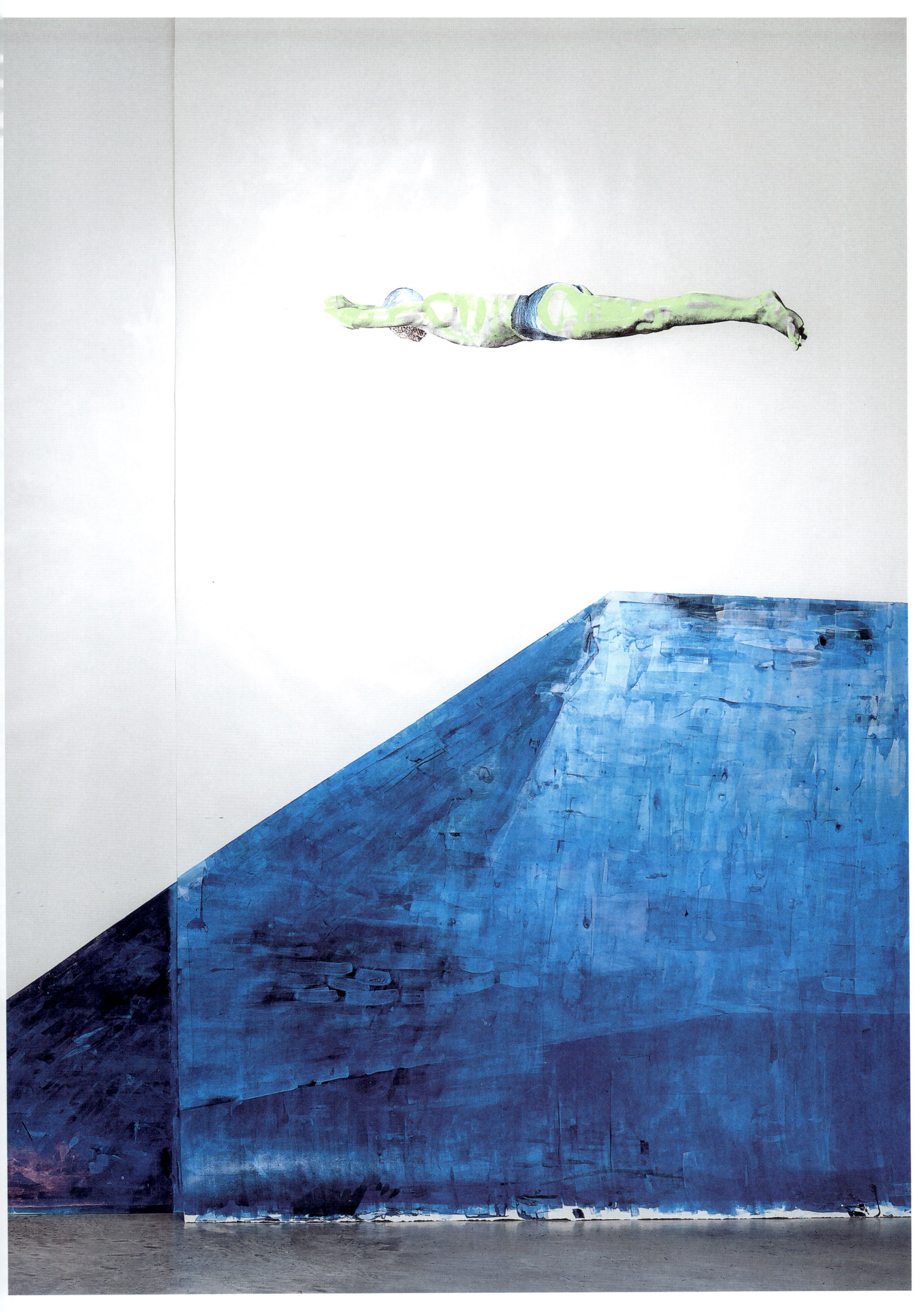

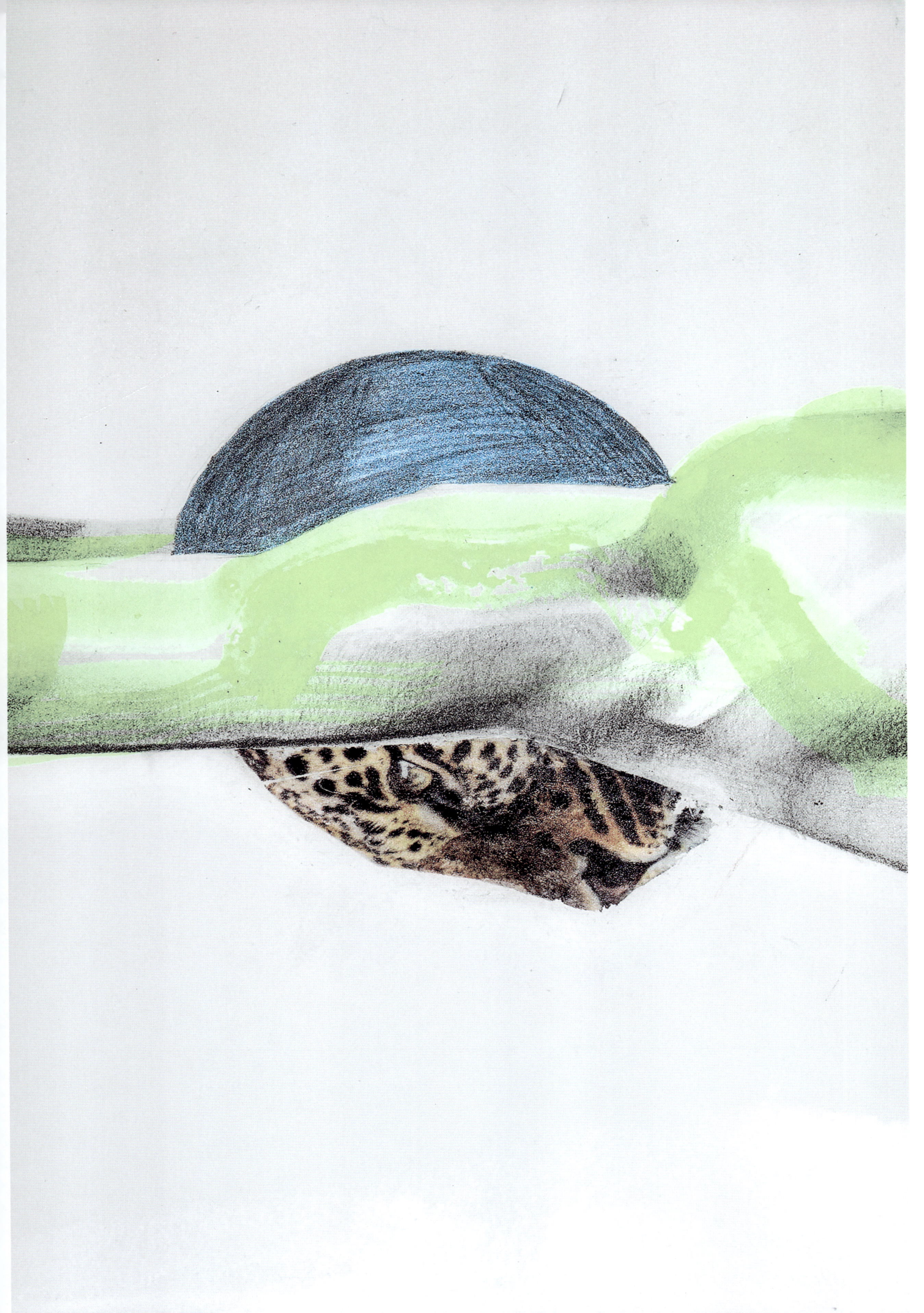

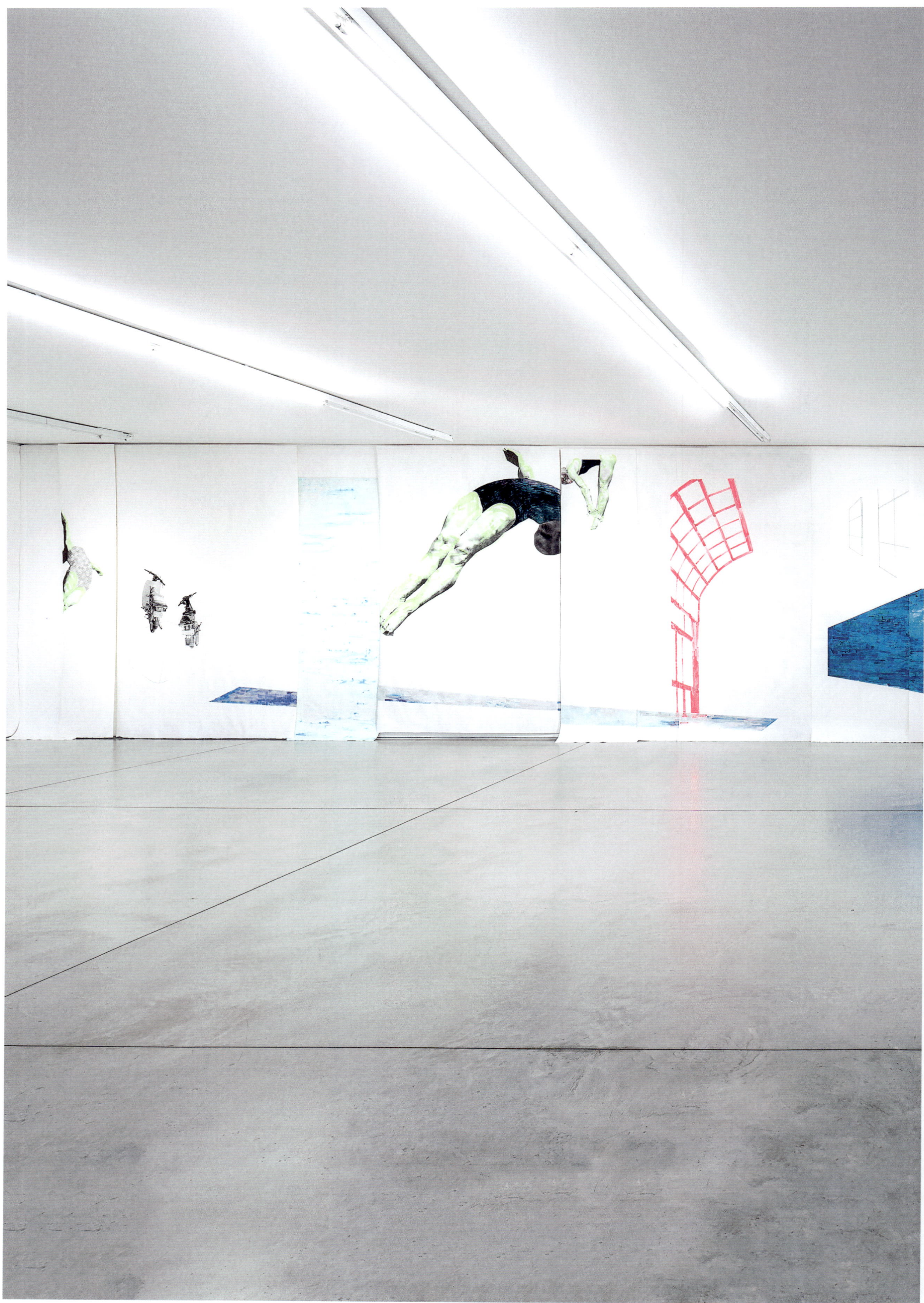

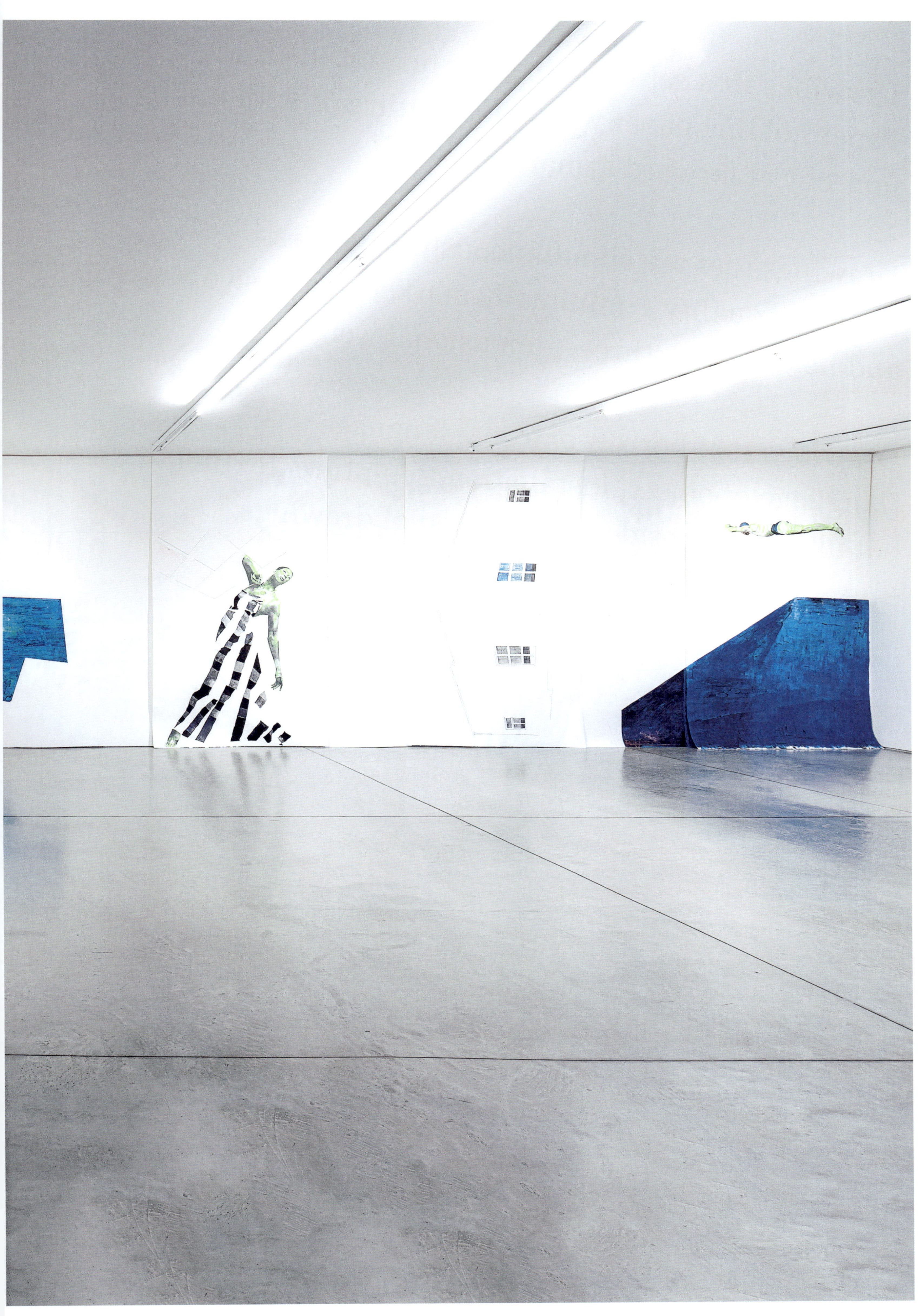

Drawings that self sustain their magnitude.
Paper holding paper without armature or with minimal,
non-object forward armatures

Drawings that are simultaneously weightless
[material quality + minimally marked, expansive paper space]
and hold spatial, three-dimensional weight

Drawings that borrow external language
[language of object, installation, sculpture, textile],
but ultimately reside in the canon of drawings.

ruby onyinyechi amanze

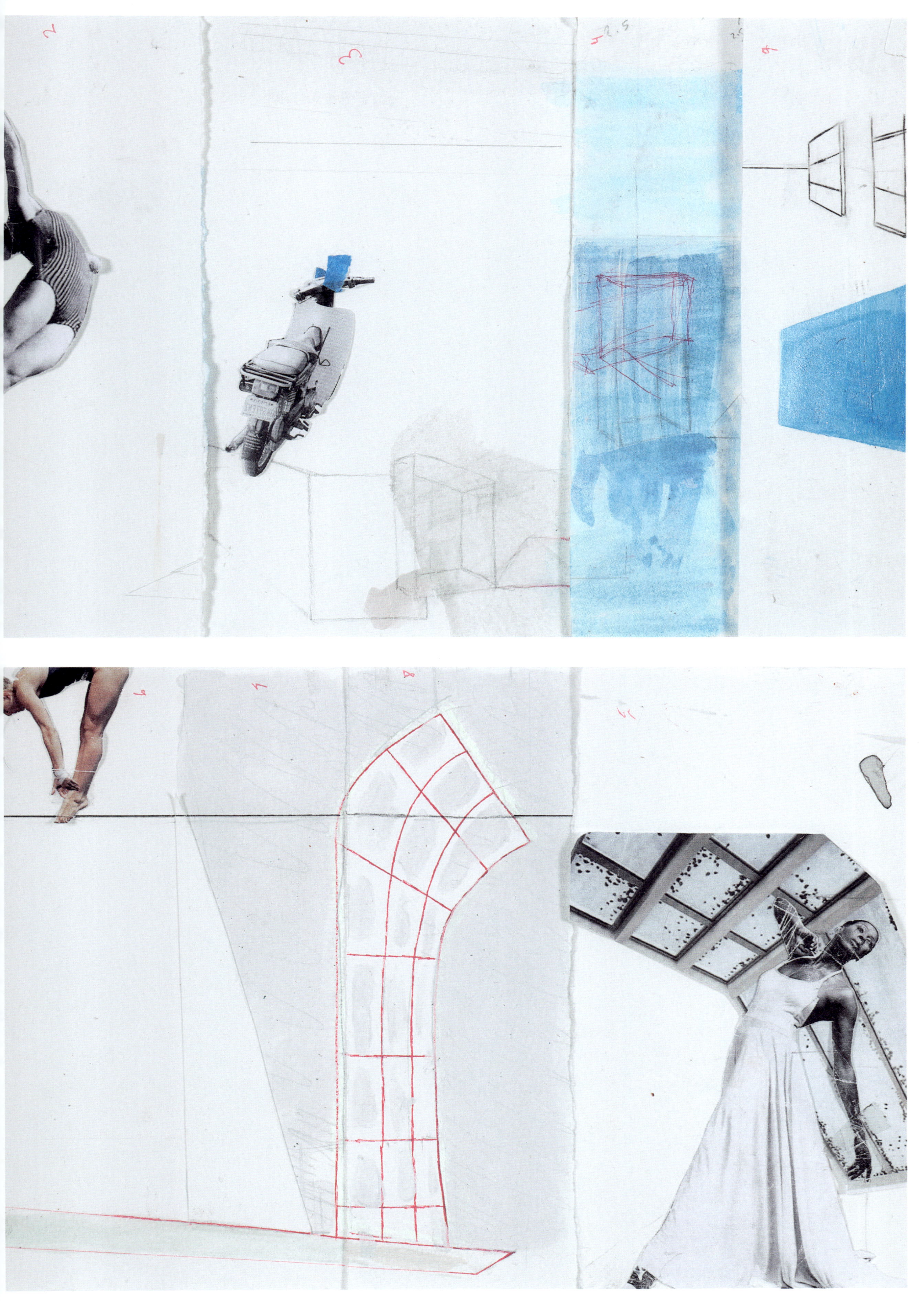

# ruby onyinyechi amanze

Born in 1982 in Port-Harcourt, Nigeria. Lives and works between Philadelphia and New York, but calls multiple places home. She earned a Bachelor of Fine Art at Tyler School of Art (Temple University, Philadelphia) in 2004 and a Master of Fine Art at Cranbrook Academy of Art (Bloomfield Hills, Michigan) in 2006.

Nata nel 1982 a Port-Harcourt, Nigeria. Vive e lavora tra Philadelphia e New York, ma considera casa molti luoghi. Ha ottenuto un Bachelor of Fine Art presso la Tyler School of Art (Temple University, Philadelphia) nel 2004 e un Master of Fine Art presso la Cranbrook Academy of Art (Bloomfield Hills, Michigan) nel 2006.

## SOLO EXHIBITIONS / MOSTRE PERSONALI

2020
*the ones that stayed*, Goodman Gallery, London / Londra

2018
*there are even moonbeams we can unfold*, Goodman Gallery, Cape Town / Città del Capo

2017
*STAR FISH*, Smack Mellon Foundation, New York

2016
*The Divers*, The Armory Show, Mariane Ibrahim Gallery, New York

2015
*SALT WATER*, Goodman Gallery, Johannesburg
*astroturf rooftop picnics*, Morgan Lehman Gallery, New York
*a story. in parts.*, Tiwani Contemporary, London / Londra

## GROUP EXHIBITIONS / MOSTRE COLLETTIVE

2020
*The Moon Seemed Lost*, Hales Gallery, New York

2019
*Drawing Biennial*, The Drawing Room, London / Londra
*you are so loved and lovely*, with Wura-Natasha Ogunji, Fridman Gallery, New York

2018
33rd Bienal de São Paulo – *Affective Affinities*, São Paulo / San Paolo
*A Slice through the World: Contemporary Artists' Drawing*, The Drawing Room and Modern Art Oxford, London / Londra

2017
*Regarding the Figure*, Studio Museum of Harlem, New York
*The Ease of Fiction*, Museum of the African Diaspora, San Francisco
*Open Sessions*, The Drawing Center, New York
*Drawing Biennial*, The Drawing Room, London / Londra
*In media res*, Diverse Works, Houston
*The Day Comes*, Galerie des Galeries, Paris / Parigi
*Nine: 2017 Studio Program Exhibition*, Queens Museum, New York
*Dialogues in Drawing*, Jenkins Johnson Gallery, San Francisco

2016
*Un-becoming*, Fridman Gallery, New York
*The Ease of Fiction*, California African American Museum, Los Angeles
*Planes and Corridors*, The Drawing Center, New York
Prix Canson 2016, The Drawing Center, New York
*New Revolutions*, Goodman Gallery, Johannesburg
*The Ease of Fiction*, Contemporary Art Museum, Raleigh
*KIN*, Hanger, Lisbon / Lisbona

2015
*Magic*, with Wura-Natasha Ogunji, Omenka Gallery, Lagos
*A Constellation*, Studio Museum of Harlem, New York
*Remember to Come Back*, Mariane Ibrahim Gallery, Seattle
*Speaking Back*, Goodman Gallery, Cape Town / Città del Capo
*No Such Place*, Edward Tyler Nahem Gallery, New York

2014
*Telling Truths, Speaking Secrets*, Bowling Green State University, Bowling Green
*(e)merge*, Nomad Gallery, Belgium, Washington D.C.
*In Sheep's Clothing*, Gallery 220, New York
*BRIC Biennial, Volume I*, Bric Arts Gallery, New York
*Mutations*, Tiwani Contemporary Gallery, London / Londra
*I See You: The Politics of Being*, Harvey B. Gantt Center, Charlotte
*Drawn Truly*, Corridor Gallery, New York

2013
Select Fair – Art Basel, Rush Arts Gallery [New York], Miami
*Six Draughtsmen*, Museum of Contemporary African Diasporan Arts, New York
*no one belongs here more than you*, Centre for Contemporary Art, Lagos
*Crossing The Line: Contemporary Drawing*, Mixed Greens Gallery, New York
Department of Fine and Applied Arts Faculty Exhibition, University of Nigeria, Nsukka

2012
*Waiting for the Queen*, Dyker Gallery, Brooklyn Academy of Music, New York
*Neither Here, Nor There*, Brooklyn Public Library Flatbush, New York

2011
*Part II*, Causey Contemporary Gallery, New York
*The Salon*, Greenpoint Gallery, New York

2010
*Paint&Print: a Portfolio Project*, Amsterdams Grafisch Atelier, Amsterdam
*Exchange VI: Contemporary Prints*, West Gallery, Purdue University, West Lafayette
*Multiplicities of Syntax*, Cora Stafford Gallery, University of North Texas, Denton
*Transforming Technology*, SGC Philagrafika 2010 Print Conference, University of the Arts, Philadelphia

2009
*One Night Stand*, Main Line Art Center, Haverford

2008
*From Taboo to Icon*, Ice Box Gallery, Crane Arts, Philadelphia
*Works on Paper*, Philadelphia Sketch Club, Philadelphia

2007
*Works on Paper*, Muse Gallery, Philadelphia
*Works on Paper*, South Shore Art Center, Cohasset

2006
*All the Things I Never Said*, Forum Gallery, Cranbrook Academy of Art, Bloomfield Hills
M.F.A. Graduate Thesis Exhibition, Cranbrook Art Museum, Bloomfield Hills
*All About Me*, Open End Gallery, Chicago

2005
*Self Location, Third Generation*, Forum Gallery, Cranbrook Academy, Bloomfield Hills

2004
*Cranbrook / Wayne State Graduate Exchange*, Community Arts Gallery, Wayne State University, Detroit

*HOW TO BE ENOUGH*
Mixed media on paper / Tecnica mista su carta
311 × 1780 cm

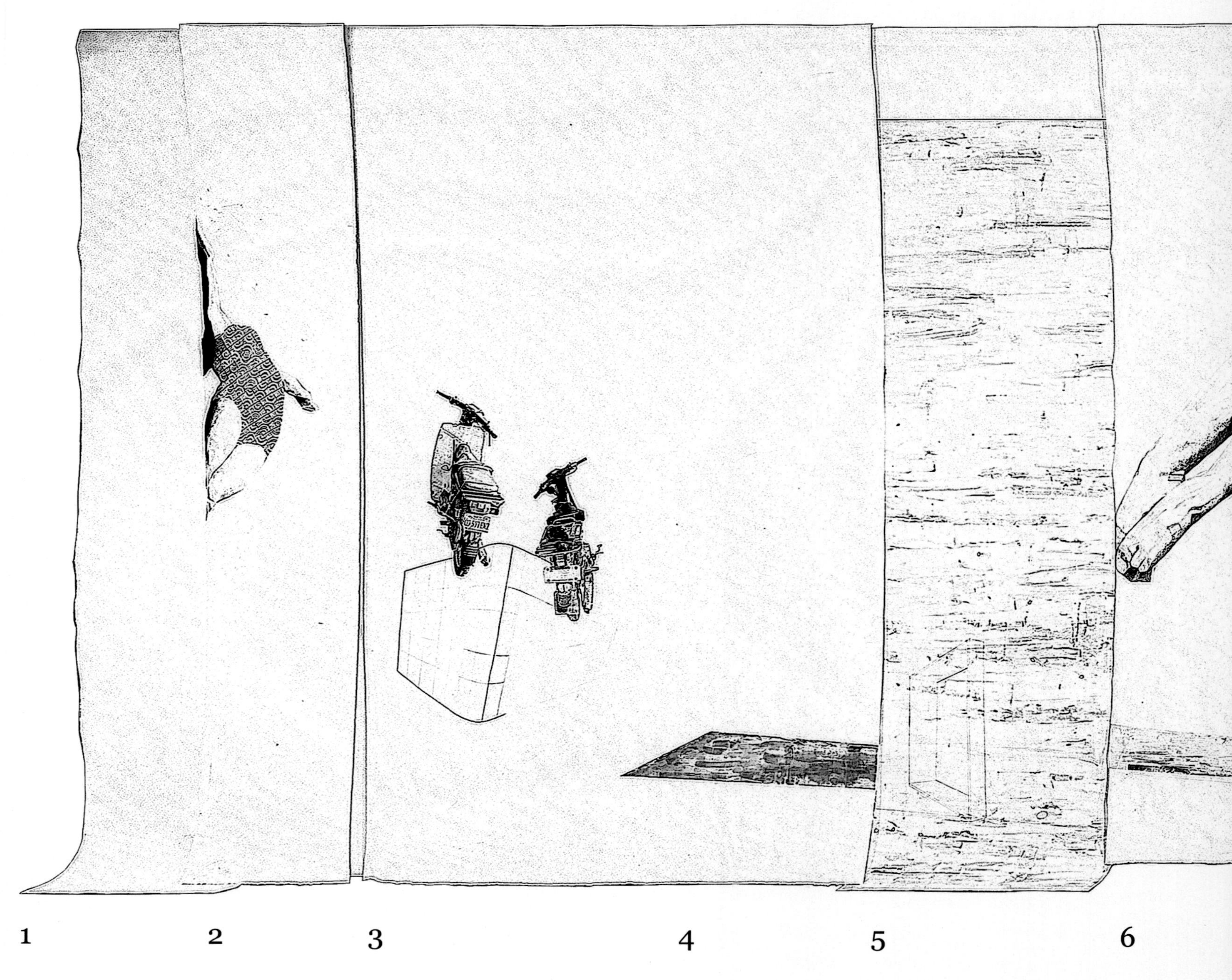

1 2 3 4 5 6

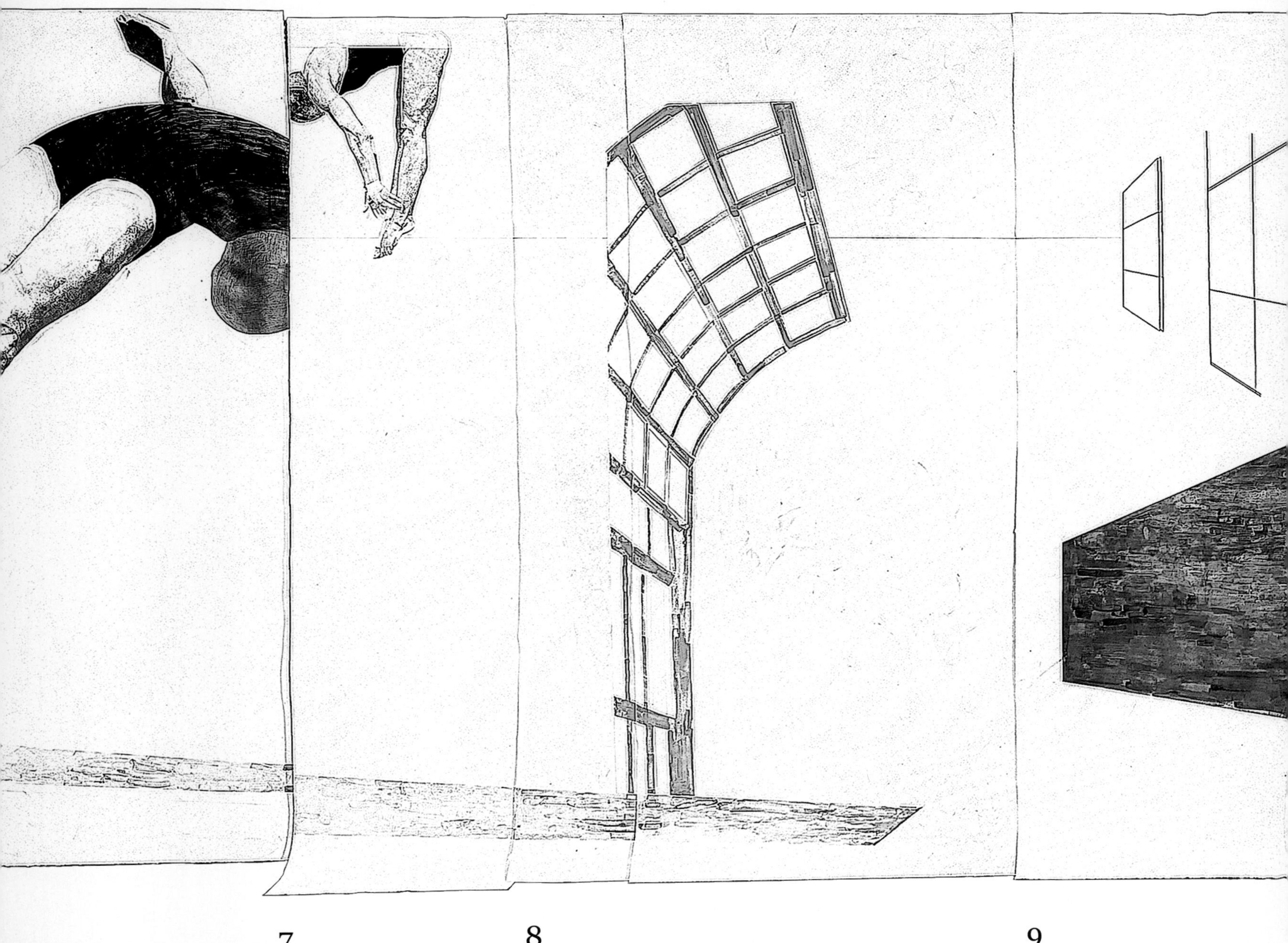

7 8 9

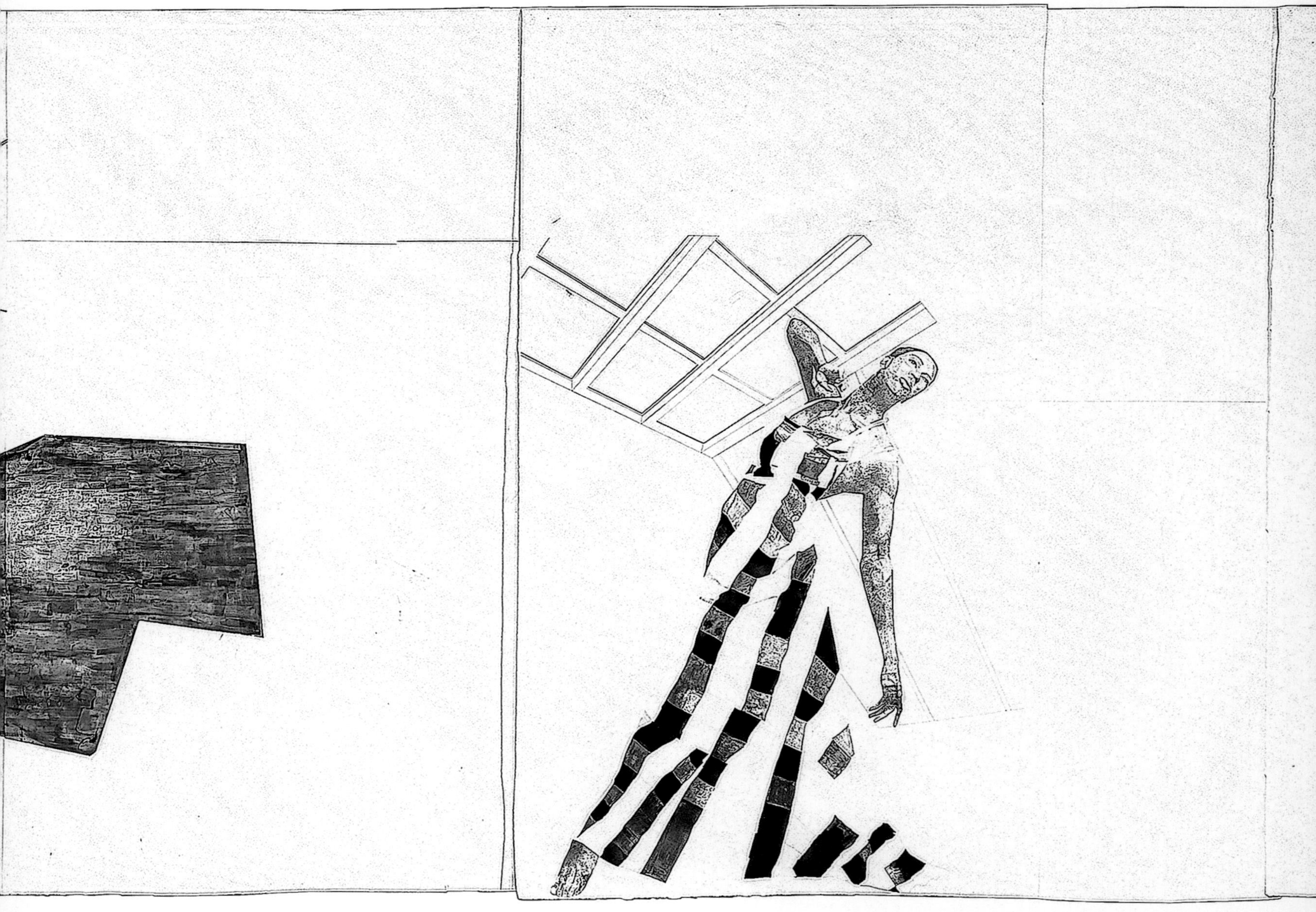

10 11 12 13

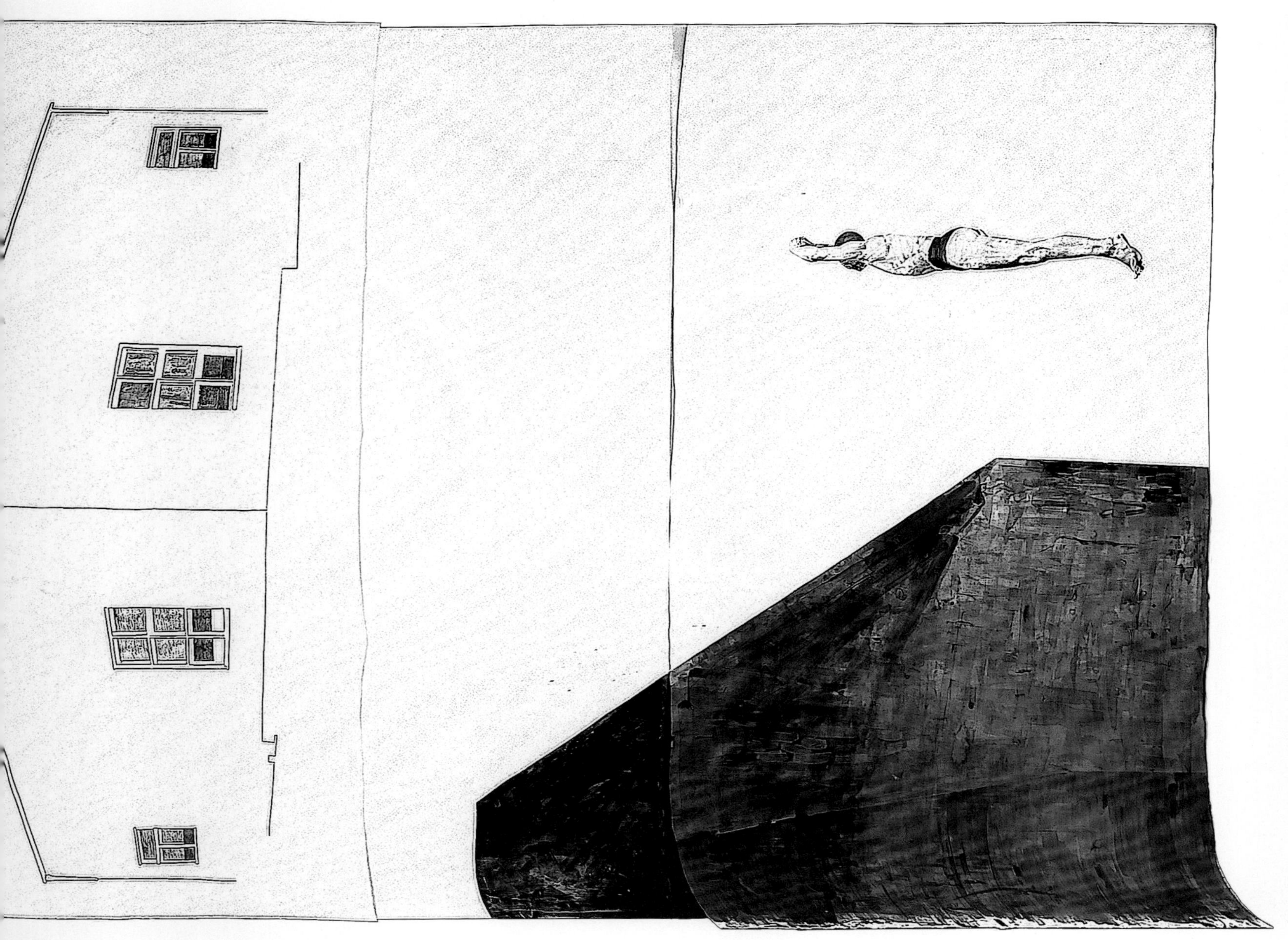

14 15

1 *LANDING INSIDE*
*[fullness, not absence]*
or *[paper]*

2 *OUT. SHE EXITED QUIETLY, BUT DECIDEDLY*
or *[ada] edge, left*

3 *WE RACE THROUGH THE STREETS LIKE ONES*
*LOOKING FOR DEATH UNPROTECTED AND FEARLESS*
*IN SPEED, THE JOY LINGERS*
or *[bikes] two*

4 *THIS IS WHERE I FIND YOU*
and/or *cap [pool, bottom]*

5 *SCORPIO*
or *[pool] deep*

6 *OVERRIDING*
*[she was wild]* or *the first. [ada].*

7 *IT WAS FROM WATER. TO WATER, WE RETURN.*
or *[ada] top, dives*

8 *MR GOLDEN SUN SPUN US AND THROUGH UMBILICAL*
*CORDS OUR EYES WERE CRYSTAL CLEAR*
*WE LANDED TO THE LEFT AND TO THE RIGHT [earth]*
and/or *[windows] grounded, reaching*

9 10 *ARRIVE AT THE BOTTOM AND BREATHE*
and/or *[windows + pool #1] travel left – right*

11 *AS GRACE [Judith] SHE ASKED, WHAT COLOR IS*
*A WINDOW? MY DARLING, A WINDOW IS CLEAR*
*OR IT'S PINK.*
and/or *[ada + windows] up. down.*

12 *WALK [selah]*
and/or *[paper] #2*

13 *HOW TO BE ENOUGH [facades]*
and/or *[windows-architecture] mirrored. upright.*

14 *INTRO [fixed water]*
and/or *[pool] #2, left*

15 *THE EXPANSE OF AUDRE [EASE OF FLIGHT]*
*[DEPTH] wings fueled by generators and palm wine,*
*audre holds us up*
and/or *[audre + pool #2] above and beneath*

# ruby onyinyechi amanze
# HOW TO BE ENOUGH
## 21.02–25.07.2021
## Collezione Maramotti

Published on the occasion of the exhibition with the same title /
Realizzato in occasione della mostra omonima.

With an essay by Mario Diacono and a conversation between
ruby onyinyechi amanze and Gaia Clotilde Chernetich /
Con un saggio di Mario Diacono e una conversazione
fra ruby onyinyechi amanze e Gaia Clotilde Chernetich.

Photographs / Fotografie
Roberto Marossi, Jeffrey Stockbridge

Acknowledgements / Ringraziamenti
ruby onyinyechi amanze would like to thank:
Zaha and James, for the love and space to draw
the Wives (fuel for fire)
the studio/thought assistants over the years, for bending paper with me
and preparing my brain for this moment: Atisha, Fileona and Gregory
Brian, for Showing Up /
ruby onyinyechi amanze vorrebbe ringraziare:
Zaha e James, per l'amore e lo spazio per disegnare
il gruppo delle Mogli (benzina che alimenta il fuoco)
gli assistenti di studio/di pensiero, che negli anni hanno ripiegato la carta con me
e preparato la mia mente per questo momento: Atisha, Fileona e Gregory
Brian, per essere comparso all'improvviso ed essere rimasto

Collezione Maramotti would like to thank Serena Trizzino for her collaboration /
Collezione Maramotti ringrazia Serena Trizzino per la sua collaborazione.

Publishing editor
Ilaria Bombelli (Mousse)

Design
Marcello Jacopo Biffi (Mousse)

Translations / Traduzioni
Marguerite Shore (It–Eng)
Aurelia Di Meo (Eng–It)

Proofreading
Lindsey Westbrook
Agnese Cantelmi (Mousse)

Published and distributed by / Pubblicato e distribuito da
Mousse Publishing
Contrappunto s.r.l.
Corso di Porta Romana 63
20122, Milan / Milano

Available through / Disponibile attraverso
Mousse Publishing, Milan / Milano
moussepublishing.com
DAP | Distributed Art Publishers, New York
artbook.com
Vice Versa Distribution, Berlin / Berlino
viceversaartbooks.com
Les presses du réel, Dijon / Digione
lespressesdureel.com
Antenne Books, London / Londra
antennebooks.com

Printed by / Stampato da
Grafiche Veneziane, Venice / Venezia

First edition / Prima edizione
2021

ISBN 978-88-6749-459-0
€27 / $30



collezionemaramotti

MaxMara